Praise for *Mind of a Champion*

"*Mind of a Champion* is an enlightening guide to enhance and align spiritual, emotional, and cognitive intelligence. This book will stimulate the spirit and ignite a passion most may not realize exists. Excellent read!"

Dr. Kimberly Hunley, Ph.D.
Corporate Consultant and University Professor

"*Mind of a Champion* is a common concept written with an uncommon approach filled with examples to help make the concepts come alive. Dr. Campbell incorporates biblical principles to explain concepts that take the reader through a unique journey of illumination!"

Ivy Chin, Corporate Executive Sr. Vice President

MIND
—— of a ——
CHAMPION
It All Starts With Your Mindset

Mind Of A Champion: It All Starts With Your Mindset
Copyright © 2017 Regina D. Campbell, Ph.D.

All rights reserved. No part of this book may be reproduced (except for inclusion in reviews), disseminated or utilized in any form or by any means, electronic or mechanical, including photocopying, recording, or in any information storage and retrieval system, or the Internet/World Wide Web without written permission from the author or publisher.

Book design by:
Arbor Services, Inc.
www.arborservices.co/

Printed in the United States of America

Mind Of A Champion: It All Starts With Your Mindset
Regina D. Campbell, Ph.D.

1. Title 2. Author 3. Self-Help

Library of Congress Control Number: 2017910680

ISBN 13: 978-0-692-91713-8

MIND
―― of a ――
CHAMPION
It All Starts With Your Mindset

Regina D. Campbell, Ph.D.

I want to dedicate this book to my parents.

My parents molded and shaped my thinking as a champion through their work ethics, teaching and being loving and caring parents. To the late H. Paul Woods who was a man of God that took of care his family, thanks dad for being a great father. I remember when you said to me "you must accept the call on your life and know God will hold you accountable for what He has assigned for you to do" thanks dad for those words will always be embedded in my heart and spirit. To my wonderful and amazing mother who truly exhibited Proverbs 31. Mom although you currently are not capable of articulating your thoughts and feelings I am grateful for all the lessons you taught me as I grew up and matured as a person. I am grateful for the many times we spent discussing life and how to navigate the vicissitudes of life. Most of all I am thankful for you always encouraged me to achieve my goals and never to stop believing with God all things are possible. Thanks dad and mom!

Contents

Acknowledgment xi
Forward xiii
Introduction xv

Chapter 1: Reframe Your Mind 1
   Section I: Our Mind Is Shaped by Our Experiences 1
   Section II: Program Your Mind to That of a Champion 4
   Section III: Stop Negative Thoughts 7
   Section IV: Focus on the Positive 10
   Section V: Fill Your Mind with Positive Messages 14

Chapter 2: See Beyond Where You Are 19
   Section I: Situations Don't Make You 19
   Section II: The Mind of a Champion 21
   Section III: Can You See What Could Be? 23
   Section IV: You Can't See Differently with a Negative Mindset 27
   Section V: See Beyond Your Past 30

Chapter 3: Know Who You Are 35
   Section I: You Were Chosen by God 35
   Section II: You Were Formed and Shaped by God 38
   Section III: God Knows You 42
   Section IV: Know Yourself 46
   Section V: Know Your Strengths, Goals, and Passions 50

Chapter 4: A Higher Standard 53
   Section I: Dedication to Excellence 53
   Section II: Stop Settling for Less 56
   Section III: The Law of Attraction 60
   Section IV: Time Keeps Moving Forward 63
   Section V: Raise Your Thinking and Your Standards 65

Chapter 5: Deliberate Living and Determined Focus 71
   Section I: Living Life with Purpose and Intention 71
   Section II: Know Why You Do What You Do 75
   Section III: A Road Map to Your Destiny 77

Section IV: Deliberate Living: Planting the Right Seeds 80
Section V: Determined Focus: Exercising Self-discipline 83

Chapter 6: Seize the Moment: Window of Opportunity 87
Section I: Tomorrow 87
Section II: Fear of Failure 90
Section III: Seize the Moment 94
Section IV: Be the Best You Can Be 97
Section V: Window of Opportunity 100

Chapter 7: It's How You Speak: Free Yourself 105
Section I: Words Can Hurt or Help You 105
Section II: You Are What You Say 108
Section III: Coordinate Your Mindset and Words 112
Section IV: Words Are Powerful 115
Section V: Speak with Faith and Assurance 119

Author Biography 123

Acknowledgment

I want to thank my husband (Reginald I. Campbell) for his love and support on this project. Your support has been unwavering as I embarked upon this daunting task. Thank you "love" for your words of wisdom, spiritual guidance and steadfast love and companionship I am immensely grateful. Most of all I am grateful to God for your strength, foresight and friendship. Finally thanks to the children (Pharez, Liz and Brandi) I pray that you will seek God for a Champion's Mindset.

I want to thank my family (sisters, brothers, nieces and nephews) you guys are amazing and I am appreciative for the love and support we have amongst each other. I thank God for His favor, grace and blessings he has bestowed upon us as a family. I am a better person because of your support and steadfast love. I couldn't have asked for a better family!

I am thankful for my church family (HOR). I thank each of you for helping me to live a champion's life through your love, prayers and support! Finally thanks to Ken Gary photographer for his support.

Forward

Dr. Campbell brings clarity to the things that often leave us confused and hopeless. Her ability to make practical the Word of God is life changing. Each chapter of this book will grab you in a way that will bless you beyond measure. This must read book will change the very mindset of those who have a bowed down head to lift it up and experience the beauty of a changed, focused, and positive mind. This book will build your faith to another level that you will truly "Walk by Faith and not by sight". Thank you Dr. Campbell for blessing our hearts and MINDS to receive the Words that will bring hope, strength, but mostly life!

Pastor Sean Dogan
Long Branch Baptist Church
Greenville, SC

Introduction

"Our life always expresses the result of our dominant thoughts."
~ Soren Kierkegaard

It is great to have goals, dreams, and hopes. And taking steps to work toward your goals is wonderful. If you do not have the right mindset, however, you may never reach your goals—not because you are unable to achieve them but because you can hold yourself back from success, often without even realizing it.

You see, if you do not have a positive mindset and a belief system that tells yourself you are capable and willing to meet and exceed your goals, then you could be doomed to fail before you even start. Failure itself isn't bad, provided you fail because you try—instead of because you never start—and that you learn from your mistakes and move forward in a positive and deliberate manner, choosing to keep going and not give up. Think about this: One's level of success is determined by one's mindset.

Greatness lies within all of us; however, only those who have a mindset of greatness will become great. The mind is the doorway to how a person thinks. What you allow into your mind is what you will focus on and become. Therefore, what you read or listen to is important. The mind is the vehicle to your emotions; how you feel about and react to what happens to you starts in your mind. Therefore, remaining levelheaded is crucial so your emotions do not go in a direction you regret, resulting in a negative mindset.

In order to have a positive mindset, you have to learn to control your emotions. For example, if you think someone doesn't like you and you ponder that thought continually, your emotions will follow. Your emotions will increase your resentment and dislike for that person. Your mind also is a container; it harbors thoughts—thoughts about people, your situation, your past, your future, yourself, doubt, fear, success, winning, and losing, among other things, so be careful what you focus on.

We should concentrate on those things that are praiseworthy and not on imperfections or negatives. Granted, this doesn't mean that you should ignore truth. However, once you have acknowledged the difficulty of a situation, then you have to decide whether to allow those negative thoughts and emotions to remain in your mind, cycling and circling through it on a continuous loop, or to ensure that positive thoughts occupy your mind. If you allow destructive thoughts, you become a victim to those thoughts, letting them control you and hold you back from reaching your God-given potential. This can be a vicious and never-ending cycle. Thus Scripture enlightens us that how we think is what we become.

For example, if someone wants to become stronger and healthier by working out, she would need to have a positive attitude and truly challenge herself. She might hire a demanding trainer to add even more of a challenge. Before workouts she could fill her mind with self-affirming messages, such as "I can do this." And while working out, if she was performing a difficult exercise, she could again tell herself that she could do it. By doing these things, she might feel strength and positivity. And, as a result, she is likely to find that she can run farther, lift more weights, and do more of a variety of exercises than ever before. Her positive pattern of thinking and belief in herself and her ability, as well as setting clear goals, are the reason she is able to live up to this challenge.

The focus of this book, as the title suggests, is having the mind of a champion. We will examine what having the mind of a champion means, how to achieve it, and how it could affect your life in extremely positive ways. Included are verses from the King James Version of the Bible, as well as a few other versions, that demonstrate the main points in this book.

We will discuss various mindsets or perspectives so you can examine your current mindset and, if needed, change it to a positive one that will help you think positively and get results. We will discuss the victim mindset and the champion mindset in detail because these two ways of thinking are almost totally opposite of each other.

If you have the victim mindset, that means that you feel and act as a victim; you do not take control of or responsibility for your life or in your failure to meet goals. Instead, you focus and put too much energy and time into having pity parties and making defeated comments about yourself or about what has happened to you. We all have experienced misfortunes, but we need to take on a victorious mindset by rising from the ashes of despair and taking on a champion mindset. If you have the victim mindset, you will find it impossible to reach your goals and to feel competent and capable.

If you have a negative mindset, you may misinterpret something that someone else says or does. If you think everyone is against you and that nothing good ever happens to you, then you'll misinterpret kindness. You may believe that no one is nice and that there is some sort of ill intention behind a person's actions or words. Watch how you interpret your life experiences; everything and everybody is not out to harm you. Even in a world of misfortunate and chaos, there are still many good people who are truly genuine.

It is my hope that you will be able to use the ideas in *Mind of a Champion* to improve your life and be the best you can possibly be. It can help motivate you, if you let it, so you will believe in yourself and your ability to meet your goals and then, because of that belief and the hard work that you put in, reach your goals.

> *Finally, brethren, whatsoever things are true, whatsoever things are honest, whatsoever things are just, whatsoever things are pure, whatsoever things are lovely, whatsoever things are of good report; if there be any virtue, and if there be any praise, think on these things. (Philippians 4:8)*

Chapter 1:
Reframe Your Mind

Section I: Our Mind Is Shaped by Our Experiences

"For as he thinketh in his heart, so is he: Eat and drink, saith he to thee; but his heart is not with thee." Proverbs 23:7

Consider this: A puppy was tied up on a chain outside for several years where he had only a limited range of movement. One day, suddenly, he was released. Even though he was no longer tied up on a chain, he continued to stay in the same limited area to which he had been confined. Why didn't he leave the area and go far away since he was now free? His mind had been conditioned and programmed to accept that he could not get away and did not know that he could run away since he was no longer tethered. People are much the same way. The ways in which we think are often determined strongly by our experiences. We are no different than the puppy who did not know he was free.

Or you may go to church and realize that you are like that puppy in that you are tied up with all sorts of issues holding you back: fear, doubt, low self-esteem, insecurity, anger, and/or mistrust from past experiences. You may have these issues or you may know someone who is held back by his or her own negative thinking.

You may wonder how you can get free from what is holding you back and keeping you from success, your destiny, and being all that you can be. How can you become free from the negative way you have thought about yourself in the past?

Our mind is shaped by our experiences, whether good or bad. If your mind is shaped by primarily bad experiences and you have a negative mindset about yourself, your life, and your capabilities, then you have to learn to think and believe positively about yourself and your place in the world. Then, even if you have negative experiences or failures in the future, you need to continue to believe good things about yourself and in the great things you are capable of.

Experiences heavily influence how we think of ourselves and our situations. For example, the way in which we've always done something can become tradition, such as the activities we do at Christmas. It might be that we've always been successful and expect that to continue. Or perhaps our experiences have taught us that we will fail at everything we do; in this case we are setting ourselves up to continue that pattern. Traditions are detrimental if you aren't free and liberated enough to embrace something better or different that happens to come along.

Our minds are also shaped by the things we were taught as a child about ourselves and the world. Even if what we were taught wasn't accurate, we may continue to believe it and act upon it. Maybe you were taught that you are always right and should always get your way. Or you were taught that you were no good, not smart or capable, or did not measure up to your siblings, so you believe that and act in accordance, making sure—consciously or subconsciously—that you fail, even when success is possible.

You may be what is getting in your way, even though you may blame the world and/or anyone else you perceive to be in the way. You may act how your mother, father, aunts, uncles, grandparents, teachers, friends, etc. taught you. Reality, of course, may be different from what you were taught.

Our minds are also shaped by our belief systems. This can include what we have been taught growing up. Your parents may have taught you good or bad work habits or how to treat elders, friends, or members of the opposite sex. Your mind and your success or failures are also shaped by your locus of control, which is a psychological concept. If you have an external locus of control, you believe that your life, your successes, and your failures are controlled by forces outside of yourself and beyond your control. An internal locus of control, on the other hand, means that you feel in control of your life and your destiny; this corresponds closely with the champion mindset.

Our minds may also be shaped by our family's history, including certain patterns of behavior such as alcoholism, chronic unemployment, college graduation, success, etc. You can either follow the trend or work to overcome it.

Section II: Program Your Mind to That of a Champion

> *"Casting down imaginations, and every high thing that exalteth itself against the knowledge of God, and bringing into captivity every thought to the obedience of Christ;"*
> 2 Corinthians 10:5

Let's first discuss what the concept of having the "mind of a champion" means since this concept is the basis of this whole book. After that, we will look at specific strategies to help you truly develop the mind of a champion or to help you maintain or improve your mindset if yours is already that of a champion.

A champion is one who wins first place in a competition or who shows marked superiority. We are not talking about being better than other people but in thinking positively to reach your goals, whatever your goals may be. A champion does not always have to win, but champions persevere. They work hard to try to reach their goals and expand their horizons and, most importantly, do not give up, no matter what adversities or challenges they face. In order to keep going no matter what life throws at them, champions must have a positive mindset. They are confident and proud—not arrogant—and feel that they are entirely capable of doing whatever it is that they set their minds to.

An excellent example of someone having the mind of a champion is Thomas Edison. He set out to invent an electric lightbulb, and he knew it could be done. Although he had to go through hundreds and hundreds of different materials to try to make the lightbulb work, he never gave up. After hundreds of failures, he finally found a filament that worked. If he had simply given up, he never would have reached his goal of inventing the electric lightbulb. (He was a determined inventor, by the way, eventually earning over one thousand patents for his work.)

Another great example of someone with the mind of a champion is Martin Luther King Jr., who tirelessly fought to increase opportunities and civil rights for African Americans. Even though he went through a great deal of adversity, including arrests and threats against himself and his family, he continued with his important work of improving lives and promoting civil rights. His tragic assassination did not diminish the progress that he made or his legacy.

Both of these people perfectly embody how people operate when they truly have the mind of a champion. They set clear goals, they kept going no matter what, and they believed they could and would succeed. Countless other people who are not famous also have the mind of a champion, everyday people who set goals and succeed, whether their goals are to help people, make it to the top in their careers, or be a wonderful parent and spouse.

The common denominators in people who truly have the mind of a champion is that they believe in themselves, they are not afraid to set goals, they do not give up, and they think in a positive manner. People who have the mind of a champion are willing to do whatever it takes, within legal, ethical, and moral bounds, to reach their goals.

Can you think of someone you know, maybe someone you have been influenced by who truly has, or had, the mind of a champion? What traits and characteristics did he or she have that demonstrated a champion mindset?

The goals can be in any variety of areas, such as starting work in a certain field, writing a book, overcoming addiction, improving relationships with family, being an excellent parent, making more money, starting your own business, or even climbing a mountain. There is no end to the types of goals you can set. With any of these goals, if you want to be successful, you need to know that you can do it.

While it might sound easy to have the mind of a champion, it is not easy for people who are used to thinking negatively and not believing in themselves or in their capabilities to change their thinking. Programming your mind to think like a champion is, however, entirely possible. If you truly have the desire to have the mind of a champion, you can do so. That may mean changing the ways in which you are used to thinking, feeling, and believing, which, in turn, will change the way you live your life and that you work to meet your goals.

Although we will discuss programming (or reprogramming) your mind more in detail, realize that it is a process of stopping your negative thoughts and focusing on the positive and on what is possible. Like the puppy mentioned earlier, you can stay tied up and unable to make progress, or you can set yourself free so you are truly able to meet and exceed your goals. The choice, even if you do not quite believe it yet, is yours.

Just because you have spent most of your life feeling inadequate and, predictably, not living up to your potential or making the progress you wanted to make does not mean you have to live the rest of your life the same way. While you will likely always face some tough circumstances in life, how you deal with those challenges and move ahead toward your goals demonstrates your mindset. Are you going to let adversity set you back? Or are you going to do what it takes, no matter what, to reach your goals?

We will come back to the idea of the mind of a champion. Next, we will discuss how people can change their mindsets and program their minds to that of a champion.

Section III: Stop Negative Thoughts

In order to develop the mind of a champion, you must stop negative thoughts. A wide variety of negative thoughts go through people's minds, such as fear, doubt, and worry. In addition, many people have negative thoughts about their own capabilities and skills. Immediately arrest or stop the negative thoughts that flow through your mind. If you ponder negative thoughts, they will continue to permeate your mind and hold you back from successfully meeting your goals. If you feed them, they will only grow.

Thoughts are like seeds in that once they are planted, if they are given nourishment (or focused upon), they will grow. The more you focus on negative thoughts and give them energy, the more they will expand. Don't feed those bad thoughts. It is possible to expand negative thinking so much that you crowd out any possible room for positive thoughts. Instead, focus on stopping the negative thoughts. This practice can be difficult, but it is definitely possible and worth the time and energy.

Here are some of the things that are negative or even harmful things that people sometimes allow to run through their minds:

Worries about:
- Self-esteem
- Health
- Looks
- Money
- Lack of previous success
- Little or no experience
- Intelligence
- Academic abilities
- Addiction problems

This list is by no means comprehensive, but it gives you an idea of the types of things that people may think. What other kinds of negative thoughts do you have?

There are several ways to try to stop the negative musings that run through your mind. You can, for example, make a list of the negative thoughts that flow regularly through your mind so you are aware of them. Depending on how often negative cognitions pervade your thoughts, you may even want to spend some time writing down the date, time, and exact thoughts that go through your mind. Self-awareness like this takes time and practice, but it may well be worth it.

Once you have catalogued all of the negative thoughts—or even one repeating, continual thought—then try to replace each negative thought with a positive one. If the thought you have is, for example, *I don't have what it takes to start my own business*, then you could try to replace that thought with, *I am going to do everything in my power to start my own business and be successful at it, even if I experience a few challenges along the way*. Try to figure out positive thoughts to replace each negative thought.

But also work on analyzing why you resort to negative thinking. Why do you, for example, have a low self-esteem? Why do you think you aren't capable of meeting your goals? Getting to the root cause of your negative thinking can also help you to replace the thoughts with positive ones. If you were told as a child and adolescent, for example, that you weren't good enough, realize that they were being unreasonable and not helping you to develop a healthy self-esteem. Then work on replacing the undesirable thoughts in your mind with positive ones.

Your actions and your success are dictated by your thoughts, so the more you believe in yourself and your capabilities, the more success you will experience, especially if you take concrete steps that will help you make progress toward your goals; we will discuss this concept in more detail later.

Another strategy to help stop negative thoughts is to talk about them with other people. Sometimes simply talking with a loved one, such as a family member, friend, or trusted colleague, about negative thoughts and why you think them can help the thoughts go away.

One obstacle that can get in the way of positive thinking is mental health issues. Not everyone who thinks negatively has a mental health issue, but some people do. Some mental health problems, such as anxiety disorders, mood disorders, depression, and post-traumatic stress disorder (PTSD), among others, can lead some to think negatively. People with addictive behaviors, such as drug and alcohol abuse, are also prone to negative thinking. If this is the case with you, or if you are not sure, consider scheduling a session with a therapist, counselor, psychiatrist, or social worker to see if you have a diagnosable disorder or if you just need help stopping your negative thinking. After diagnosis, you may find that therapy, medication, or a combination of both help you to decrease or eliminate your negative thoughts.

Another idea to stop negative thoughts is to do something active, such as go on a walk or work on something concrete toward your goals. Find what works for you. By finding some strategies to stop negative thoughts, you will be well on your way to developing the mind of a champion.

Section IV: Focus on the Positive

Focusing on what is good will help take your thoughts away from the bad, the negative, and the undesirable. You may have already written down or talked about your negative thoughts; now you should write down or talk about some positive thoughts. If you focus on the good first, you will be less likely to focus on the bad. Maybe your previous negative thought was, *I will not be able to earn my college degree because I am not smart enough.* Now you can replace that with a positive affirmation: *I can graduate from college, I am very capable of doing so, and I will not stop until I complete my degree.* Think, write, or state this until you believe it.

Following are some other examples of specific negative thoughts that can be replaced by positive thoughts:

Old, negative thought: *Why should I even bother taking this new job? I've never had any luck with jobs before. I've either gotten fired or disliked the job and quit. I'm sure the same thing will happen with this new job.*

New, positive thought: *Great! I've got a new opportunity to try a new job that I'm sure I'm going to love! I'm going to work hard, do my best, and take advantage of this chance.*

Old thought: *I'm a failure. I never do anything right. I've had a drug addiction, my relationships have not worked out, and I don't have any idea what to do to make my life better.*

New thought: *I've made many positive choices and improvements in my life. Although it wasn't easy, I was able to overcome my drug addiction. I've learned from past relationships and now have a better idea about how to make them work and to choose better people to be involved with. I'm ready to move forward and feel confident about being successful!*

Old thought: *I want to learn about graphic design, but it's pretty complicated for someone as unintelligent as I am.*

New thought: *I have learned many new things before, and I can learn much more. Graphic design sounds fascinating! I can't wait to get started.*

Old thought: *I am going to be trapped in this low-paying, boring job forever! I doubt I could get a better job. Even though I dislike this job, I am better off just staying with it. I've been here for three years with no raise and no promotion, so why should I think that will change?*

New thought: *If I work hard and look out for new opportunities, I am sure I can find a better job than this one. Or I could work to get promoted within this company. I always have options.*

As the above examples illustrate, part of the problem may be the way in which you interpret or perceive things that happen to you. Do you, for example, see something challenging as an obstacle or as an opportunity—to learn, to grow, to expand your horizons and push yourself? Whether you look at something as an obstacle or an opportunity says something about your tendency to be negative or positive.

Try viewing obstacles as opportunities. If you get fired or laid off from a job, for example, use it as an opportunity to try something else. The world will not end, for example, if someone with whom you are in a romantic relationship decides to end the relationship. While this may hurt you temporarily, and may, in fact, be extraordinarily emotionally painful, use what seems like a problem as an opportunity to decide if you want to date or marry someone; if you do, set decisive goals about what you want and are willing to put into a relationship. Getting out of an unhealthy or unbalanced relationship can be a great, progressive step forward, even if it does not seem like it at the time.

If you are trying to follow a diet and exercise regimen but you get off track, don't get too discouraged. Use it as an opportunity to learn. Analyze why you got off track, which could mean that you stopped eating healthily or that you did not exercise as regularly, and try not to let the same thing happen again. If your boss gives you more work or extra responsibilities, take that as a compliment, and use the extra responsibilities as a way to learn more and feel even more confident about your capabilities.

When you face struggles and problems, do you view them as all negative or as something that can help strengthen you? Use the pain you experience to help you become stronger and to become your power. Focus on God's ability, not the situation or your inability.

Consider all the things that God did in the Bible that seem miraculous. He turned two fish and five loaves of bread into food for five thousand people. He was able to turn water into wine. Just because He wished it so, the world came into existence. You are God's creation. You are an amazing being who has the God-given ability to be successful and reach your goals. Be the best you can be, and don't hold yourself back!

Remember that the Creator is not subject to nature—instead nature is subject to its Creator. If God has created the universe and everything in it, including you, and if everything God has created is miraculous, aren't you also miraculous and highly capable of thinking positively, setting goals, and being successful? Again, focus on the positive. The more you do so, the easier it will be for you to see what is positive, about you, your situation, your potential, and your life. Focusing on the positive will help you to develop the mind of a champion.

Section V: Fill Your Mind with Positive Messages

Your mind is extremely powerful. You can choose, by your thoughts and actions, to help yourself or hurt yourself, to help others or hurt others, to make the world a better place or a worse place. Much of what happens to you begins in your mind. Think of it as a door or filter. Whatever you let in that door will, of course, get in and influence your other thoughts. The enemy can attack your mind. If you filter what you allow yourself to focus on, then you can shut the door in the face of the enemy.

One way to help yourself get over negative thoughts is to inundate your mind with positive messages that flood out negatives ones. For example, fill your mind with scriptures from the Bible that build your faith. Focus on thanking God first and praising Him for what He is doing or what He has already done for you. The Word of God can be your personal defense against negative thoughts, which turn into less than positive beliefs and actions. Below are some examples of scripture that have positive messages that can help you if you focus on them.

Psalm 46:1 lets us know that we always have the Lord to draw on for strength and help.

God is our refuge and strength, a very present help in trouble. (Psalm 46:1)

Isaiah 40:31 reinforces the idea of the personal power and strength that is to be found through God.

But they that wait upon the Lord shall renew their strength; they shall mount up with wings as eagles; they shall run, and not be weary; and they shall walk, and not faint. (Isaiah 40:31)

We may sometimes forget that God is in our corner and will help us in times of need, as Exodus 14:14 tells us.

The Lord shall fight for you, and ye shall hold your peace. (Exodus 14:14)

While reaching our goals is important, it is also important to do this without being jealous of or desiring what other people have. Knowing this and knowing that God is always there for us, as we help ourselves to be successful, is a useful message, as we are informed in Hebrews 13:5.

Let your conversation be without covetousness; and be content with such things as ye have: for he hath said, I will never leave thee, nor forsake thee. (Hebrews 13:5)

Psalm 23:1 tells us that God is guiding us in the right direction and will help to meet our needs.

The Lord is my shepherd; I shall not want. (Psalm 23:1).

> One step in the right direction, according to Psalm 84:11, is doing the right thing.

> For the Lord God is a sun and shield: the Lord will give grace and glory: no good thing will he withhold from them that walk uprightly. (Psalm 84:11)

> Our ability to do what we have promised or planned is reinforced by Romans 4:21.

> And being fully persuaded that, what he had promised, he was able also to perform. (Romans 4:21)

In Numbers 13:30, the message is that God's people are capable of overcoming challenges and obstacles.

> And Caleb stilled the people before Moses, and said, Let us go up at once, and possess it; for we are well able to overcome it. (Numbers 13:30)

Here, as we have been discussing, in Proverbs 23:7, the Bible lets us know that you are what you think about and what you believe in your heart.

> For as he thinketh in his heart, so is he: Eat and drink, saith he to thee; but his heart is not with thee. (Proverbs 23:7)

Or you may fill your mind with other types of positive messages. Here are some of the other types of messages that you may find help you:
- Personal mantras, such as "I am capable and intelligent" or "I am beautiful"
- Goals and how you plan to reach them
- Positive thoughts about yourself and your abilities
- Compliments other people have given you
- Successes you have experienced in the past to give you confidence about what you can accomplish in the future

Also keep in mind that surrounding yourself with other people who are positive and who give off good energy will help you to also be more positive. You may find people in your life that you need to stay away from because of their negativity. People who constantly complain about everything or who criticize you unfairly, for example, are people you should avoid as much as possible. While being around people who are negative may help fill your mind with hurtful thoughts and messages, being around those who make you feel good will help to bring you positive energy and, in turn, positive thoughts.

In whatever way you need to, whether with inspirational Bible verses, verses from other religious texts, personal mantras, or something else, focus on filling your mind with positive messages. You can't help but become more positive if you expend your energy on messages that are uplifting and beneficial. If you realize how powerful negative thinking can be, then you also should realize that positive thinking is equally powerful if you give it the focus and attention it needs to be able to make a big change in your life. By focusing on the positive, you will be on your way to being more confident and to taking concrete action toward meeting your goals.

Chapter 2:

See Beyond Where You Are

Section I: Situations Don't Make You

The ability to see beyond the obvious is important. Seeing beyond is related to having vision instead of simply looking at what is in front of you; you see what is possible and what could be.

The following Bible verse relates directly to the concept of seeing beyond.

For we walk by faith, not by sight. (2 Corinthians 5:7) This next Scripture addresses the eternal quality of faith and having vision.

While we look not at the things which are seen, but at the things which are not seen: for the things which are seen are temporal; but the things which are not seen are eternal. (2 Corinthians 4:18)

Situations are temporal, which means that they are related to time. Most situations are not permanent. In many cases, just because you don't like how things are now in your life does not mean that you cannot work actively to change things.

Keep this in mind: Situations don't make you . . . you make the situation.

This does not mean that people can control and change every single situation they are in. People have little control over war, chronic illness, etc. But a vast majority of situations can be changed. Following are some examples of situations that people may find themselves in that they, ultimately, have created. Try to put yourself in these situations.

Bad grades: Maybe you are in college, working on whatever degree you have chosen, and you find that the work is too hard. You never had to work this hard in high school to make good grades; in fact, you were able to maintain an A or B average in almost all classes there. At this university, however, you have mostly Cs and Ds in your classes, except for the A you have in the one class, your favorite class, that you don't have to do much other than show up. In your other classes, you are frustrated by trying to keep up with your assignments. You are mad because you have failed or made poor grades on tests. Papers that would have gotten you As or Bs in high school earn poor grades in your college classes. Your classes are boring. Some of your professors are nice, while some are strict, inflexible, difficult to talk to, and uninterested in excuses. You enjoy spending times with your newfound friends and do not intend to spend every second studying. You do your assignments right before they are due. Sometimes you dislike going to class; sometimes you don't even go.

In the above situation, the student has created his own circumstances as far as poor grades and negative attitude go. This student could take responsibility for earning better grades instead of blaming others and not trying his best. He could make sure to learn the study skills that he did not pick up in high school. He could view his university classes as the chance to get an education and a privilege instead of a chore. He could easily take control of the situation that he got himself into.

In order to live your life the way you want, you must take charge of it and live according to productive goals and principles.

You must decide if you will let what you see in terms of situations and experiences dictate your thoughts, beliefs, and actions. You must take control of your own destiny, changing your mindset to that of a champion.

Section II: The Mind of a Champion

People who have the mind of a champion have several characteristics that help them to succeed. First, these people are confident and believe strongly in themselves and in their abilities. They know they can do it. Second, they are focused on and are not afraid to set bold goals. Being goal-oriented helps them to direct their energy and time in the areas that will help them succeed. Third, they do whatever it takes to meet their goals, provided that what they do does not hurt other people or themselves and that what they do is within ethical, moral, and legal bounds. They show a great deal of perseverance, even when challenges and difficulties get in their way, which often happens when people are pursuing goals. Fourth, they think in a positive way, focusing on the good and not allowing negativity to invade their thoughts and cloud their judgment. They are realistic but not pessimistic. All of these traits put together are what make up the mind of a champion. We will continue to discuss strategies and ways that you, too, can develop a champion mind.

Here are some things that you must know related to having a champion mind:

- You must learn to know that there is more to you than you may know. You are a complex being with a wide variety of talents, abilities, and interests. You may even have talents that you have no idea about yet just because you haven't tried them or haven't had the opportunity.
- You must know that God has more in store for you that you do not realize yet.
- You must know that where you are is not destiny; there is more to come, provided that you do what you need to do to make things happen. Just because you may not be exactly where you want to be now does not mean that you have to always stay that way. People sometimes make the mistake of failing to look to the future or of not having hope. Have hope. Have determination. Know that where you are is a step on the way to your final destination.
- You must know that there is more to learn and more to know. Having the mind of a champion means that in addition to being willing to do what it takes, you have to be willing to learn new things and develop new skills. If your dream is to become a politician so you can make the world better, you must learn how to effectively interact with all sorts of people; you might even want to take classes in or earn a degree in political science along with learning in-depth information about the areas in which you want to try to make improvements.

- You must look at your present, see beyond where you are, and desire more for yourself and more for your family. This does not mean that you should desire more material things (not that there is anything wrong with having the things that you need and working to obtain nice things, as long as that is not your main focus); it means that you should focus on fulfilling your dreams and being the best person that you can be.

With the mind of a champion, you'll have more revelation, greater insight, and a keener understanding of how to make your life what you want it. As you have already learned, your mind is shaped by your experiences, good or bad. You must change your mindset to that of a champion, stop negative and depressing thoughts, focus sharply on positive thoughts and beliefs, and inundate your mind with positive messages. You've also learned that your situations do not create you; you, alternatively, create your situations. As we continue, we will look at even more strategies and specifics about developing the mind of a champion and, thus, creating the life that you want.

Section III: Can You See What Could Be?

With the mind of a champion, you can learn to see what could be.

As this next verse shows, God can do truly amazing things, and you can too!

The hand of the Lord was upon me, and carried me out in the spirit of the Lord, and set me down in the midst of the valley which was full of bones, And caused me to pass by them round about: and, behold, there were very many in the open valley; and, lo, they were very dry. And he said unto me, Son of man, can these bones live? And I answered, O Lord God, thou knowest. Again he said unto me, Prophesy upon these bones, and say unto them, O ye dry bones, hear the word of the Lord. Thus saith the Lord God unto these bones; Behold, I will cause breath to enter into you, and ye shall live. (Ezekiel 37:2–5)

God is asking you:

Do you think you can get that degree?

Do you think you can truly eat healthy?

Do you think you can get that job?

Do you think you can be set free from a horrific past?

Do you think God can help you?

God can take what looks dead and give it life.

The question is not if God is able; God is definitely able. And so are you!

Can you see it?

Can you see a better future?

Can you see a different you?

Can you see a better you?

Can you see God's power living in you?

Can you see what could be?

Following are some different scenarios that require some thinking beyond to see possibilities, hope, or a way out.

One person might be working a job at a factory, a job that he considers to be boring and mindless, although at least it pays decently. He dislikes going to work. He only does it, of course, like many people, because he needs the money. It is just one more meaningless job he has had. He has to work because he must pay his bills, such as rent and the child support for his children. He doesn't know of any other type of work he could do, and, to be honest, he hasn't tried very hard to find anything interesting.

He is interested, however, in history and politics. He wasn't ever great at school, but he does have friends and family who would help him, academically and emotionally and with a job search after college. Maybe the reason he does nothing to change his situation is because he is afraid of major change or thinks he could not be successful in college and then at finding a professional career. The same thing, day after day, week after week, has him feeling bored and depressed, but he keeps at it.

In the above situation, what could the man do? He is bound by the belief that he can't do anything to change his situation and that he might not be successful. So far, he cannot see what could be; he cannot see all the possibilities. Change is hard work, and so is seeing what could be. Here are some things he could do: He could keep working at his present job long enough to save up money and then go to a college or university. He could even keep the job while attending college, either in person or online.

Once he graduates from college with a degree, perhaps in history, he would probably find that the job market and his opportunities within it are substantially increased. Maybe he could work at a museum, as a tour guide or curator; with his new degree, he would have many different possibilities. He might even decide that he enjoyed college and learning so much that he wants to earn advanced degrees. He could, if he wanted, live somewhere nicer once he earned his degree, or he could stay where he is if he is happy there. Probably, since he suffers from depression, he should see a therapist to help him with that and with his other issues. All of these possible solutions are possible if he has the vision to see what could be and develops the mind of a champion. With a newly developed positive perspective and a sharp focus on his goals, he could make his life the way he wants it to be.

Another situation in which people find themselves is being involved in one or a series of unhappy relationships. A woman might have been in different failed relationships all of her life so far. She may have gone from one unhealthy or even abusive relationship to another, sometimes being the one being abused and sometimes being the one who was emotionally and verbally abusive. In some of the relationships, both she and her boyfriend may have been abusive to each other. While she is willing to end relationships, she always seems to jump right into another relationship, quickly and without getting to know the person well enough.

In this situation, there are things this woman could do to improve her situation. She could get out of her current relationship and spend some time out of a relationship, not dating or becoming involved with another man. She could realistically analyze her relationship history to see why she always gets involved in relationships that are not positive or beneficial. Of course, she could also talk to friends, family, and maybe even a therapist to examine her relationship history. Writing in a journal might also help her sort through the facts and feelings and come to some conclusions. With her next relationship, she could make sure that she and the man she wants to date are truly compatible and could work hard to make the relationship a success, one that is healthy for both people involved. Consequently, she also could develop the mind of a champion and could see what could be.

Section IV: You Can't See Differently with a Negative Mindset

"One cannot alter a condition with the same mindset that created it in the first place." Albert Einstein

As the Bible verse below illustrates, new things require new ways and new methods of doing things.

No man putteth a piece of new cloth unto an old garment, for that which is put in to fill it up taketh from the garment, and the rent is made worse. Neither do men put new wine into old bottles: else the bottles break, and the wine runneth out, and the bottles perish: but they put new wine into new bottles, and both are preserved. (Matthew 9:16–17)

You can't see differently if you have the same mindset. Seeing differently requires a change in attitude, change in mindset, and a change in how you do things. Change can be difficult. Some people resist change, even when situations will most likely change into ones that are more positive. You decide on your mindset, so choose a positive one.

Having a negative mindset will cloud your vision. When you have a negative mindset, if you are in a situation that you do not like or if you haven't met your goals or reached your potential, you may decide that things will always stay the same or will probably get worse. If you have a negative mindset, you must get rid of it or you will be unable to develop the mind of a champion and to reach your true potential. You can follow all the other advice in this book and still not be where you need to be if you retain a gloomy outlook. Things just will not work if you don't first change your perspective.

If you've graduated from college, gotten a job in your field, and are married, for example, but are unhappy with your career, you won't be able to see differently with a negative mindset. You will, again, either think things are set and can't change or that they will get worse. You won't realize the potential you have to change careers altogether, work for a different company, find a different job in your field at your current company or at another one, or go into business for yourself. You won't realize that you can also go back to school or learn another trade if you need or want to.

Many people have New Year's resolutions and goals, and around January 1 many people solemnly swear that they will keep their New

Year's resolutions. They tell friends and family of their plans. They may even do what they resolved to do for a few days, weeks, or even months, but eventually, most people seem ultimately to give up on their New Year's resolutions. It is easy to decide that, for the next year and beyond, you are going to eat healthy, exercise more, get published, stop arguing with your family, go back to school, pursue that new career you've been interested in, or finally give up drugs and alcohol.

But once the gloss of a new year wears off, you may decide to postpone your resolutions, decide you can't make the resolutions happen, or even forget about your resolutions altogether. If you decide you can't make them happen, you are demonstrating a negative mindset, and with that, you will be unable to see differently. Setting goals is easy, but following through and making them happen is the hard part. You must show strength, positivity, courage, and perseverance, among other traits, to turn resolutions and goals into reality.

The challenge with New Year's resolutions and with goals in general is that many people have not changed the way they think. They may have a moment of clarity where they realize that things need to change, but if they continue to think negatively and mentally process in the same manner they always have, they will have a hard time seeing how things could be different.

You might decide that you are, after all these years, leaving the corporate rat race and going into business for yourself. Easy to say, but not so easy to do. You might decide, once you start looking at all the things you would have to accomplish and complete to make this happen, that you aren't up to the task. You will simply keep working and disliking your career because the alternative, going into business and being your own boss, is simply something you cannot do.

You may have decided for New Year's that you are going to lose weight, eat better, exercise more, and get in shape. Instead of setting concrete goals and following through, however, once you are faced with the same unhealthy but tempting foods, you partake, deciding that it is simply too hard not to. When you have the opportunity to exercise, you decide that you will do it later or not at all because you don't have the energy and endurance. You tell yourself you can't keep this up, you've have always had issues with weight; thus it's too hard to change. See how easy it is to set a goal but not follow through? See how easy it is to be unable to see things differently because of your negative mindset?

A new behavior comes out of a new mindset. Changing your behavior and reaching your goals will likely happen only when you change the way you see things. You can't see differently with the same negative mindset.

Section V: See Beyond Your Past

Depending on what your life has been like so far, you may or may not be stuck in your past. Sometimes your mind is "stuck" on what happened to you or what someone did to you and you can't get past it.

Many things that have happened in the past can still affect people. You could have been abused in a variety of ways, such as physically, emotionally, etc., as a child, teenager, or even adult. You could have had an unhappy marriage with frequent fights and maybe an ugly divorce, including custody battles. You could have been involved in a failed marriage or in numerous unhealthy relationships. You may have had major altercations with family members that caused them to be alienated from some or all of their family. You may have had legal problems, maybe going to prison for drug possession or assault.

If you are stuck in the past and can't move beyond it, you are not helping yourself or anyone else by remaining in that dark place. You are, in fact, giving power to whatever person or event causes you such grief and torment. Instead, decide to take back the power that your past has over you so that you can move forward, develop the mind of a champion, and succeed.

Does the parent who was abusive, the spouse that you divorced, or the friend who betrayed you deserve your thoughts and energy because of what they did to you in the past? Do the drug addiction you had years ago, the loss of a loved one in the past, or an unreciprocated love interest from a long time ago need to still haunt your present?

If you can move beyond whatever it is that has happened in your past that is holding you back, you will free up much more of your energy to devote to developing a champion mind, formulating goals, and succeeding at those goals. Like freeing up space on a computer's hard drive by getting rid of old programs and apps so that you can use that space for new items, once you let go of the past, you will be much closer to living in and succeeding in the present. The key to possessing a mind of a champion is moving past your past. Don't allow misfortunes, mishaps, mistakes, bad decisions, or negative experiences paralyze you. The past becomes the university to learn about who you are and what you're made for. It's not for you to stop living, dreaming, hoping, and striving for a brighter day. The good news about your past is that an amazing future awaits you.

You must change your thinking and get out of your past in order to change your future. This is also hard work, like ridding your mind of negative thoughts. If your past has a powerful hold on you, you have to work to release its grip. You will then feel freedom, capability, possibilities, and potential that you may not have felt before. If you must dwell on part of your past, dwell on the successes you have experienced and the good times you've had; you can find them if you look hard enough.

Get rid of those things that hinder you. Bad memories of the past are one of those things. Your past may influence your present with memories, less than desirable behaviors, or bad habits. Eliminate behaviors that keep you down or hold you back, and replace them with productive ones. Decide, once and for all, that your past does not and will not have a hold on you. Let it go.

Letting go of your past may take a lot of work, and no one is suggesting that this is a simple or quick process, but it is necessary in order to develop the mind of a champion. You might think, for example, of successes you have had and positive experiences in your life to replace the bad parts of your past you have focused on. You want to deal with the bad things in your past, but then you owe it to yourself and your loved ones to move on.

If you think of yourself as a victim, then you need to lose that mindset. Instead, think of yourself as an overcomer. Whatever happened in your past is over. Yes, you may have at one time been a victim of child abuse, but now you have survived that. You are strong and courageous and should think of yourself in that way.

Instead of thinking that you can't do whatever it is that you have set as a goal, think that you can do all things through Christ, who strengthens you, and through your own personal strength, and with the support of your loved ones.

There are various ways that people can work to overcome their past. They can write about these events to help get their feelings out so they can move forward. They can discuss these events with supportive and understanding friends and family. They can see a therapist to discuss their feelings and thoughts to help them progress, which could mean that they are involved with individual, family, or group therapy. They could also join a support group for people who have had similar negative experiences, which could be helpful as long as the group is committed to helping its members deal with the past and move on.

To have the mind of a champion, you have to dream big, think big, and believe in yourself and your capabilities. Once you can see beyond where you are and can get beyond negative thoughts and your past, then you will need to truly know and understand who you are. That is what we will examine next.

Chapter 3:
Know Who You Are

Section I: You Were Chosen by God

To develop the mind of a champion, you must reframe your mind to stop negative thoughts, focus on positive thoughts, and then see beyond where you are now, visualizing yourself meeting and exceeding your goals, whatever they are. In this chapter, we will discuss the importance of knowing who you are. If you do not truly know who you are, you'll have a difficult time being happy and successful, setting appropriate goals, and living your dreams.

We were chosen by God, according to this Scripture:

> *Ye have not chosen me, but I have chosen you, and ordained you, that ye should go and bring forth fruit, and that your fruit should remain: that whatsoever ye shall ask of the Father in my name, he may give it you. (John 15:16)*

This means that we are all handpicked and selected by God, so we are God's own. You should feel special and unique, knowing you were chosen by God.

Greek translations of the Bible use the word is *eklegomai*, which has to do with God choosing us. This word does a great job of illustrating how we are specially chosen and set apart by God. This word does not seem to have an exact equivalent in English, but the following illustration does a great job of showing how God, in fact, did choose us.

When Jesus chose his disciples, he chose a few select individuals out of many different people. If we choose to, we also can be disciples of God, specially picked by Him for whatever purpose he has for us. He depends on us to find out what our purpose is and to go for it. It may take a great deal of time and effort to figure out what your purpose is, but it will be worth it in the end!

While we didn't choose God, God chose us. That is true, according to the following Bible verse:

> *But ye are a chosen generation, a royal priesthood, an holy nation, a peculiar people; that ye should shew forth the praises of him who hath called you out of darkness into his marvellous light; (1 Peter 2:9)*

If we were chosen by God, that must mean that we are special and unique and that God chose us for a particular purpose. It means that he gave us special strengths. It is up to us to find and utilize our strengths and passions, as we will discuss further. We have freedom of choice, the free will to choose to use our potential and also the free will not to use our gifts. A person with the mind of a champion will take the time and effort to recognize, appreciate, and fully utilize the talents and gifts given to him or her by God.

It is useful for you to know that you were chosen by God, especially at times when you may feel inadequate, average, or not special. These feelings are common ones that many people experience at one time or another. Following is one example of that.

James grew up in a religious household with parents who were strict Christians. He went through school being socially awkward, sometimes finding it hard to make friends. In addition, although he had mathematical intelligence, learning disabilities made school and life in general difficult. Also, his parents physically and emotionally abused James. As a result of these problems, he developed addictions to drugs and stole from family members to get money to buy drugs. His family no longer trusts him, and he continues to take drugs and live a difficult life, working menial jobs that he does not enjoy. His belief in God has become superficial because he has become jaded through his life experiences. Although he still believes in God and often attends church, he has often questioned whether God truly exists and has also failed to realize that he is unique, special, and chosen by God.

Alternatively, here is an example of a person realizing that she was, in fact, specially selected by God.

Susan is a middle manager with a company that makes clothing and other textile items. She does not have the same education that some of her coworkers do, but she does have a tremendous work ethic and a strong sense of persistence. In addition, she is extremely knowledgeable about her job and the jobs of the people whom she supervises and her coworkers and managers; she also has a deep understanding of the company. Although she had a difficult childhood, with a distant mother and an alcoholic father who divorced when she was young, and although she lived in poverty and had to begin working full time as a teenager, she has worked hard to get where she is at this point in her life. She has been married for over twenty-five years and has two children and two grandchildren, all of whom are doing well. Susan regularly attends church and believes she is unique and was chosen by God to fulfill her mission in life, which is related to taking care of her family and enjoying the work she does, even though it is challenging.

It is up to you whether you reject or embrace the idea that you were chosen by God. Embracing the idea will help bring you closer to having the mind of a champion. You were not only chosen by God; you were formed and shaped by God, which we will examine next.

Section II: You Were Formed and Shaped by God

God created, formed, and shaped you.

> *Before I formed thee in the belly I knew thee; and before thou camest forth out of the womb I sanctified thee, and I ordained thee a prophet unto the nations. (Jeremiah 1:5)*

You were fashioned by God. God created and shaped you with a purpose and a plan in mind. He gave you special abilities and strengths. You may easily discover your talents, strengths, and interests at an early age, or you may not discover what you are good at and what your passions are until later in life. Either way, it is up to you to determine what you are passionate about, to set your goals, to have the right mindset of a champion, and to work hard to reach your goals, all of which are related to the way in which you were specially fashioned by God.

You were handcrafted by God. You have been specially designed by God. Like an item made at a specialty shop, you are a designer-made, one-of-a-kind human being. There is no one else like you! You could compare yourself to almost any item that is specially made and of which there are no others. Sometimes celebrities or other people with an abundance of money, for example, have a uniquely crafted home, a pool shaped in a certain way, clothing made only for them by world-class fashion designers, etc.

Believe it or not, you are much like uniquely made furnishings and clothing since there is absolutely no one else exactly like you. There is definitively only one you, so that makes you special. God saw to it that you were created in that manner. It is now up to you to take advantage of the wonderful opportunities you have to develop the mind of a champion, to become the best that you can, to pursue happiness, and to live out your dreams and meet or exceed your goals. You are empowered to do all of this; the choice is yours!

Your uniqueness is something to be appreciated! There may be a person somewhere who resembles you or acts like you, but that person is not an exact match. No one is totally the same as you, with the same thoughts, personality, talents, skills, experiences, opinions, etc. Even if you have an identical twin, you and your twin are unique and different, with each one of you having your own God-given talents and abilities.

You are authentic and important. Don't hold yourself back because of nagging, repetitive negative thoughts that run through your mind. As we have discussed previously, you may think that you are not good enough, capable enough, smart enough, lucky enough, or deserving enough to be all that you want, but the truth is that you are. The real and authentic you can be masked by many things, including drug and alcohol addiction, other addictions, unhealthy relationships, doubt, fear, and low self-esteem. Realize that God chose, shaped, and formed you and that you are an awesome human being capable of achieving great things!

One thing that sometimes holds people back from truly achieving the mind of a champion is low self-esteem. If you have low self-esteem, work on improving it so that you feel better about yourself and so that you know you have extraordinary capabilities if you will tap into them. Understand that God chose you, formed you, and created you, and know that you have the ability to pursue your goals and passions in life.

Just as there is a specific reason that you were chosen by God, there is also a specific reason that you were formed and shaped by God. It is, again, up to you to figure out what that reason is, to figure out what your passions are in life, and to go for them.

Following is an example of someone who understands how she was chosen, formed, and shaped by God and who has successfully pursued her passions, truly exemplifying the mind of a champion:

Kristen started out in life with many challenges. She grew up in a poor but loving family. She had a great deal of difficulty in school because of her learning disabilities. For many years in school she was not engaged or interested. She did not get in trouble but had difficulty concentrating, completing assignments, making good grades, and generally succeeding academically.

Finally in high school when she was assigned to a drama class, which she did not choose, she discovered her passion for acting. After spending the first few years of her life struggling with self-esteem issues, she finally realized that acting, being on a stage in front of an audience and really getting into a role, made her feel happy and alive. This helped her realize how unique she was. Kristen then set her goals, including making a living in theater and taking on challenging roles. She worked hard to go to auditions, which included some rejections, and was able to successfully land parts. She ended up getting parts in plays, doing community theater, and even participating in a couple of Off-Broadway performances. Besides demonstrating the mind of a champion, she has come to realize how she was formed and shaped by God.

Even though Kristen realized and deeply understood that she was formed and shaped by God, she took the initiative to reach her own goals and determine her own destiny. So can you!

Section III: God Knows You

If God created, formed, and shaped you, it also stands to reason that God knows you. He actually knows everything about you. He knows what your capabilities are. He knows if you are meeting your potential or if you are wasting it. He knows what you have done, and He knows what you need to do in order to reach your goals. He knows whether you believe in yourself or not. He also knows that you have the ability to develop the mind of a champion.

While he knows all of these things about you, he has given you the free will to choose whether or not to take control of your life and your destiny. Changes that you want to happen in your life will usually not happen without you taking concrete action. It is up to you to decide what to do and to take action when you decide what to do with your life. Part of knowing what to do with your life, however, is truly knowing yourself. Take advantage of the opportunity to know yourself, but realize that God knows you.

This Scripture does an excellent job of illustrating how well God actually knows you.

> *O lord, thou hast searched me, and known me. Thou knowest my downsitting and mine uprising, thou understandest my thought afar off. Thou compassest my path and my lying down, and art acquainted with all my ways. (Psalm 139:1–3)*

So, God knows all about you. He created you, and He has spent time getting to know you. He knows your positives and negatives. He realizes how your life has been so far. Even if you don't always understand your thoughts, He does. God knows you as well as, and even better than, you know yourself. Being understood by friends and family, and by ourselves, is significant; even if you feel like no one understands you, which most people have felt at one time or another, take solace in the fact that God knows and understands you.

As this next Scripture, which is a later section of the verse above, shows, God also knows your imperfections and weaknesses.

> *My substance was not hid from thee, when I was made in secret, and curiously wrought in the lowest parts of the earth. Thine eyes did see my substance, yet being unperfect; and in thy book all my members were written, which in continuance were fashioned, when as yet there was none of them. (Psalm 139:15–16)*

Everyone has weaknesses; that is nothing to be ashamed of. You were created, shaped, and formed by God with both great strengths and areas of opportunities; that is no accident. As we will discuss later, you should know your own personal strengths and weaknesses. Then you should work to hone your strengths and improve your areas of opportunities or learn how to appropriately manage them so they will not become detrimental to the point of negatively impacting you in various areas of your life. Keep in mind that focusing only on your areas of opportunities will hold you back from success. It is good to know what you can improve on, but if you dwell on that and do not recognize your amazing strengths and tremendous potential for success, you will have a difficult time developing the mind of a champion.

Here is another Scripture showing that God does know you well and that he has a plan for you.

> *For whom he did foreknow, he also did predestinate to be conformed to the image of his Son, that he might be the firstborn among many brethren. (Romans 8:29)*

According to this and many other Scriptures, you are formed in the image of God and His son, Jesus Christ. What does that tell you? Among many things, it can tell you that, if you were formed in their image, you must be special, unique, and full of potential. Thinking about that may help you to realize what a gift your life is and how truly blessed and awesome you are!

As you can see from this next Scripture, God indeed has a specific plan for you.

> *For I know the plans I have for you, declares the Lord, plans for welfare and not for evil, to give you a future and a hope. (Jeremiah 29:11, ESV)*

This means that God has made plans for you and your future and life so that you will prosper. However, it is up to you to figure out what your life will be and whether or not you will reach your goals, develop the mind of a champion, and be all that you can and want to be. Even though He knows what will happen in your life, just as He knows all about you, He has graciously given you free will. Free will means that all the choices about your life, your mindset, and your success and happiness are up to you. There are, of course, circumstances that sometimes occur that are beyond our control as humans. But the fact remains that we have free will and can decide what to do or not to do with our lives. Take advantage of this awesome control that God has given you over your life and make it something extraordinary!

God knows whether you are meant to be a great writer, a leader in the field of mathematics, a respected caretaker for your family, an accomplished architect, or a conscientious heating and air-conditioning technician. He knows if you have what it takes to help the homeless on a full-time, volunteer basis. He knows if you have the ability to do great things and meet your goals but are not living up to your potential.

If God can know this much about you, it makes sense that you can also discover everything that you need to know about yourself, your perseverance, and your abilities. It is up to you to discover your talents and passions, to formulate goals, and to make your goals a reality. You have free will to shape your life, but with that free will that God has given you, you also have great responsibility to develop the mind of a champion, live your dreams, achieve your goals, and make a difference in the world.

As you can see, the fact that God, who created, shaped, and formed you, knows you and has a deep understanding of you is extremely significant. In line with that, as we will discuss, it is equally important that you know yourself. Knowing yourself is a great way to take advantage of the vast freedom that God has given you to control your destiny.

Section IV: Know Yourself

"When you know yourself, you are empowered. When you accept yourself, you are invincible."

Tina Lifford

God knows you, but do you know yourself? Knowing yourself means that you have taken a deep look at yourself, who you really are, your strengths, your weaknesses, and your life, including your past and present. Knowing yourself also means examining possibilities for your future. It means knowing what type of person you are and the person you can become. It means understanding where you came from, where you are now, and where you are going.

People may not intrinsically know themselves well for a variety of reasons. Some people simply do not take the time to think deeply about and reflect on themselves. They haven't reflected on how they felt when something happened to them. They haven't explored why they responded to certain life experiences as they did. Getting to know yourself means becoming totally real and authentic with yourself; it means not being afraid of looking deeply into your soul and getting in touch with your inner thoughts and feelings. You have to know what makes you do what you do. Life can be busy, so reflection can be difficult, but it will be worth it.

On the other hand, some people are afraid to examine themselves too closely. They are afraid of who they really are and of facing their true inner self. That fear can uncover some level of pain and hurt, but the beauty of looking within is the opportunity to address and deal with buried issues from the past that continue to surface.

Following is an example of a person who, for various possible reasons, has not examined herself closely and does not seem to know herself well:

Sandra is married and has four children. She has a semiprofessional job. The one thing that seems outstanding about Sandra is her talent; unfortunately, that talent involves making other people mad and continually having ongoing problems with others. If she isn't in an argument with her husband or one or more of her kids—who have learned to avoid her when she is angry and combative—then she is in some intense interpersonal conflict with a friend or relative outside her immediate family. She is the type of person who cannot usually keep friends for too long because she drives most people away. Sandra is defensive, irrational, argumentative, and cannot ever accept responsibility for her part in conflicts. Her family does their best to stay away from her as much as possible; her kids go see their friends frequently and her husband often works late.

She wonders how life can be so difficult, yet she cannot or will not take responsibility for her own part of her problems. What is clear is that she does not know herself well or is not willing to acknowledge her challenges. Whether she needs therapy, honest self-reflection, assertive truths from her friends and family, or to be on some type of medical intervention is not clear. Until she gets to know what the reasons are for her behaviors and makes changes accordingly, her relationships and life in general are unlikely to improve.

How do you get to know yourself? Some people get to know themselves better through expressing themselves, such as through art or writing. Other people take various objective and/or subjective assessments. Yet other people focus on what other people say about them; while this may not always be accurate, what several people tell likely holds some truth. Some people get to know themselves better through therapy or counseling by exploring themselves, their thoughts, their actions, and their interactions with other people. Still other people immerse themselves in nature by walking on the beach or hiking on trails. Other people meditate. If you need to know yourself better than you already do, you will be able to find a method that works for you.

You should know your own personal strengths and weaknesses. Also, work to hone your strengths and improve your weaknesses. If, for example, you know that one of your weaknesses is staying organized, then you might want to consider ways to help you stay better organized. Staying organized is a strength that can be important in terms of success and in day-to-day life to improve productivity.

Following is an example of a person with an organization issue:

Jason is creative and talented. Besides being an artist, he is also an office manager for a mental health provider. He works hard and accomplishes a great deal; however, his organizational skills are lacking. If he were better organized, he would likely accomplish even more. He has a few four-drawer file cabinets, but he does not use the space within them wisely. A few of his files are organized well, but not many of them are. His desk is cluttered with all sorts of documents and piles of papers. Sometimes he accidentally loses important paperwork, such as billing tickets from clients' mental health sessions; when this happens, the business loses money. In fact, this has happened a few times in the past few weeks. He sometimes gets stressed out looking at the clutter in his office, but that is just how he has always done things. He even made a wonderful spreadsheet on the computer to better organize client information, but somehow he even misplaced that. He does get along well with his supervisors, coworkers, and clients. Overall, he does a good job, but if he were better organized, he would do better; he does not seem to make this connection, however.

In the above example, if Jason was more aware of his shortcomings and knew his strengths and weaknesses better, he would be in better shape. While he knows somewhat that his disorganization hurts his performance, he does not realize how much of a difference it could make. If he spent some time examining himself and his work habits more closely, he could do something about it. His supervisors could also help prompt him to examine this more carefully. He could decide to utilize the help of an organizational expert, or even the help of another colleague who is well-organized, and learn how to do better.

As you can see from this example, knowing yourself, acknowledging, admitting, accepting, and doing something about a challenge or problem enables you to grow and develop.

If you don't truly know yourself, then it is hard to know what you do well and what you don't do well. It can be difficult to discover what your true passions are if you do not really understand thoroughly who you are and what you are made of. And it can be hard to improve your personal relationships, such as those with friends and family, as well as your professional relationships. In some instances, people know themselves but do not admit or acknowledge their weaknesses. They sometimes make excuses or blame others for their behavior. Those that possess the mind of a champion are open to receiving critical and candid feedback or looking within and admitting their areas that need development. They then work hard on becoming a better person and improving in those areas of their life.

Section V: Know Your Strengths, Goals, and Passions

Knowing yourself can be beneficial in several ways. In order to develop the mind of a champion, you must know yourself, including your strengths, your goals, and your passions. Having the mind of a champion also means that the goals you set are realistic. This does not mean that you should not dream big. However, your dreams must stem from your innate abilities and be realistic if they are going to be worthwhile for you to focus on.

If, for example, you want to become an engineer but do not have the skills needed, such as a deep understanding of math and science and strong analytical skills, then you should reconsider this dream to find a goal that better matches your innate abilities and skill set. If you simply have some gaps in your understanding of math and science, then you could work to improve them. But if you are truly weak in these areas, then you should probably consider other options.

Equally important is passion. If your goal is to be an engineer and you have all the required strengths but absolutely no real interest or passion except that you want the money you would earn, then you should choose another goal. This is an example of why it is vital that you know and have a true picture of your strengths, passions, and goals.

Knowing your strengths means knowing what you are good at and not good at. It also means knowing your strengths and what you can improve. You may have learned what some of your strengths were through your schooling and education; maybe you were always good at math or at writing. In addition, you may learn what some of your strengths are through your work experiences, other life experiences, and/or hobbies. Skills that you might not always consider, such as the ability to work well with people, often called soft skills, can be as important as more concrete abilities, such as artistic talent or mathematical aptitude.

Equally important as knowing your strengths is having a solid grasp of your goals. Goals, to people with the mind of a champion, serve as a road map to where they want to go. You may well find that a large goal that you have also has multiple smaller goals that you intend to reach that are steps along the way to your ultimate goal. If you are interested in a career in business management, for example, and want to someday run your own business, you may break this down into several smaller goals; you might earn a degree in business management, complete an internship in the field, work for several types of businesses—or for a particular type that you are interested in—pursue professional development, pursue management positions as they become available, and, after you have enough experience, open your own business. Having a goal is often the first step in reaching success.

Also vital, besides goals and strengths, is knowing what you are passionate about. You may already have a clear grasp of what you feel passionate about, you may learn what you are passionate about through your experiences, or you may even find something you are passionate about but did not know you were as you discover your strengths. Life experiences sometimes help people discover their passions, which may change over time. If you are inspired by an author, you may decide to become a writer yourself. There are almost limitless things about which you can be passionate.

Next, let's look at having a dedication to excellence, an important trait for one with the mind of a champion.

Chapter 4:
A Higher Standard

Section I: Dedication to Excellence

Part of having the mind of a champion is having high standards for yourself as well as a total dedication to excellence. This means that you should always push yourself to do your best, especially when it comes to meeting your goals and fulfilling your dreams. You can have the strengths, goals, and passion to fulfill your dreams, but without high standards and a fierce dedication to excellence, you may not be successful.

According to the next Scripture, the Lord will give you strength and will lift you up.

> *The Sovereign LORD is my strength; he makes my feet like the feet of a deer, he enables me to tread on the heights. (Habakkuk 3:19, NIV)*

It is up to you to take this strength and elevation that God will give you and do what you need to do to take advantage of this. God will give you strength and lift you up, but if you don't take action, you will not progress and meet your goals. Having the mind of a champion is knowing that you must do your part and that you personally must be dedicated to excellence.

In the following Scripture, we see that God will, if we allow Him to, lead us on the path to excellence and high standards for ourselves.

> *But covet earnestly the best gifts: and yet shew I unto you a more excellent way. (1 Corinthians 12:31)*

As with the other Scripture, God can lead you on this path to excellence and achievement only if you follow Him. He will not do the work for you; you must do it yourself!

Let's review what we've learned so far about having the mind of a champion, which is a detailed and complex process. This will help you to think about the work that you must do to meet your goals, work that you should strive to do with the highest standards and strongest dedication to excellence possible.

In order to have the mind of a champion you first need to reframe your mind. Because your mind is formed by your own personal life experiences, you need to take action to change the way you think and to reprogram your mind to that of a champion. This includes stopping negative thoughts that repeatedly go through your mind, focusing heavily on the positive, and filling your mind with positive messages to counteract and act as an alternate to negative messages you may have been used to focusing on.

Next you need to take an honest look at where you are in your life and then look beyond that to the future to the almost limitless possibilities in store for you. Remember that negative situations do not make you who you are; the way that you react to situations is much more telling. You should strive to react in a way that helps you progress and overcome obstacles. Think about what you are truly capable of. With a negative mindset you will not be able to see things differently, or at least in a more positive manner. Even if you've had a difficult past, look beyond it and use it to help you grow. Remember that you were chosen, formed, and shaped by God, who knows you and what you are capable of. Make sure that you also know yourself and your unique passions and strengths; also make sure that you have a good grasp of your goals and what they require. All of this will help you to develop the mind of a champion.

Following is an example of a person with high standards, the mind of a champion, and a steadfast dedication to excellence:

Roberto wants to be an excellent soccer player. This is something that he has always been interested in. When his brother and sister played soccer on a team, when he was in elementary school, he decided that he wanted to be a part of the sport. He began practicing with his brother and sister, attending their games, and learning as much as he could about the game. He found that he was skilled and passionate about soccer, so he made it a goal to play soccer the best he could. He would often go to the soccer field and practice with his siblings for hours. When he went to middle school he tried out for the same team that his brother and sister had been on and was thrilled to be accepted onto the team. He'd probably practiced more before joining the team than any other new players.

While also keeping his grades high, Roberto played soccer and practiced as hard as he could all the way through middle school and high school. He always tried his best, kept a positive attitude, and showed good sportsmanship. In fact, when he went to college he was good enough that he earned a soccer scholarship that paid most of his tuition. He played throughout college, enjoying soccer, his studies, and his friendships. When he graduated from college he continued to play soccer and to improve his game on a community team as he began his career in architecture. As you can see, Roberto demonstrated high standards, a dedication to excellence, and the mind of a champion.

In the next section, we will examine the other side of having high standards and a dedication to excellence. That is the fact that people sometimes settle for less in their lives and from themselves than they should. Overcoming that is another important step toward developing the mind of a champion.

Section II: Stop Settling for Less

Sometimes people settle for less in their lives, in various ways, rather than going for the best. This manifests itself in various ways, such as in relationships, educational attainment, careers, and living situations.

For example, a particular young man was extremely intelligent. He earned a scholarship to attend a prestigious university. However, when he commenced his journey of obtaining his bachelor's degree, he didn't put the time into his studies, skipped classes, and didn't take the opportunity seriously. He would hang out with people who also didn't study or take college seriously. He eventually was academically dismissed from the university, and he decided to go back home and get a job.

After some years passed he realized that he had settled for short-term gain and not a long-term investment. Think about the people with whom you choose to surround yourself: do they bring out the best or the worst in you? Are these people, overall, assets or liabilities? The people you choose to surround you should in some way add to your life; you, on the other hand, should add to their lives as well. The amount of give and take in a relationship should be balanced.

Take an honest assessment of the people you are connected to and with whom you choose to share your time and your life. Evaluate each relationship. Is it toxic and poisonous, or beneficial and positive? Think about what you are striving for and what your standards are, and figure out if the people in your life are ones who will help you reach your goals, and you theirs, and are up to the high standards you have set for yourself.

In terms of education, don't settle for simply earning a high school diploma; instead, pursue higher education, as in most cases it can provide you with more career options and a higher salary than only a high school diploma. Not everyone desires to attend college. If this is true for you, then acquire a skill or trade that will provide you with a career. For example, having an electrician's license or welding license could position you for a lifelong career. Sometimes people find that, even though they didn't have much interest in elementary, middle, and high school, that they become interested in college once they take specialized courses of interest to them because of the major they have chosen.

As far as careers go, there are many reasons why people may choose to stay in careers they don't particularly like. They may think that they cannot possibly get a better job. They may feel comfortable in what they are doing, even though they have dreams of a more satisfying career. Or they may be afraid to leave their job or to try something different, either because they are afraid to try something new and possibly fail or because they are afraid that they cannot get another job.

Sometimes, however, taking a risk can lead to a better situation than a person had before! For example, Oprah Winfrey took a risk when she ended her talk show after twenty-five years in Chicago and moved to Los Angeles to start her own television network station named "OWN." John Legend, after graduating from college, took a management consultant job that lasted three years before he pursued a full-time career as an artist. Finally, Bishop T. D. Jakes left the comfort of his home state of West Virginia and moved to Dallas, TX, to pastor the Potter's House. Each of these people took a risk and are now in better situations than before. But more importantly, they didn't settle but instead reached for higher heights in their careers and spiritual destination.

Following is another example of someone who left a job in pursuit of a career in the field she felt passionate about, refusing to settle for less:

Amber had worked as the manager of a photo shop in a drugstore for several years. Although she liked the job okay, she found it stressful and tedious at times. At other times, she grew tired of the "interoffice politics" of the place, of employees who were difficult and managers who were not supportive. Her pay was not great, but it was not terrible. She wasn't terribly unhappy, but she found she was not thrilled to go to work every day. Her real interest, she had decided even before she graduated from high school, was going into the medical field. So, she decided that remaining at her job was settling for less than she wanted.

Soon, she went back to school and got licensed to be a certified nursing assistant, still working her full-time management job. Soon after, she applied for and got a job as a nursing assistant at a local hospital, working in the emergency room to help patients. Even though the pay wasn't much more than what she was earning at the drugstore, she loved this job and felt passionate about it. She also enjoyed continuing her education through professional development, even though she had not been a very interested student in school.

Amber decided not to settle for less. If you feel you are settling for less, you can do something, like Amber, to reach your goals and make your dreams come true as you develop the mind of a champion.

If you realize that you are settling for less, try to stop doing so. Stop settling for mediocre when you can do better. Stop settling for any less than the best in everything, in all areas of your life, including in your relationships and with yourself. If you are settling for less, then you may well realize, after some honest reflection, that what you are today is not sufficient to achieve your purpose. Mediocrity is the enemy of greatness!

After evaluating your life choices, are you settling for less? If so, work to change that as you move toward developing the mind of a champion. If not, that is great! Next, we will examine a concept that can help to bring positive change to your life, or to keep things positive in your life: the law of attraction.

Section III: The Law of Attraction

What exactly is the law of attraction? It means that we, in essence, create our own realities. Because God gave us the power of free will, we are able, in many cases to do this. We attract what we want, and sometimes what we do not want, into our lives through our thoughts, beliefs, and actions. What we attract can be positive, negative, or neutral, depending on our areas of focus. If you don't want anything better than what you have already, then according to the law of attraction, you will not attract anything better. If, however, you are striving for excellence and want to improve your life, in terms of your career, your relationships, your financial situation, or your own personal well-being, you will be much more likely to do so; you will attract positivity.

The following Scripture relates to the law of attraction:

> *Iron sharpeneth iron; so a man sharpeneth the countenance of his friend. (Proverbs 27:17)*

What this means is that if you are around friends or other people who are positive and can motivate and inspire you to improve, you may well do so. And, on the other hand, you can help to influence your friends and family to reach higher and improve if you give them encouragement and positive messages.

Another part of the law of attraction is that you must actively work to create the reality you seek. Wishing for and visualizing your ideal life are not enough; you must be active in making sure that the life you want is the one you have.

In order to make the law of attraction work, you should remove yourself from relationships with "basement-minded" people, those who harbor and give off only negativity, those who put you and others down, who live with chaos in their lives, who are unproductive and lackluster, and who lack vision, passion, and zeal. These are the types of people who will only bring you down. You can always try to encourage people like this to be more positive, but it is not always possible. Instead, get around people who challenge your thinking and actions in a positive way and who will help you grow in directions you want to grow, people with whom you reciprocate this positivity.

Here is an example of the law of attraction working in a negative way with someone who clearly does not have the mind of a champion:

Grant has been having difficulties in his life for as long as he can remember. Things have never been easy for him, and they seem to be getting worse. He frequently complains to his few friends, family, and coworkers, or to anyone else who will listen, about almost everything in his life. Grant notices that people in his life often seem to distance themselves from him, but he cannot figure out why they would want to do this. He and his coworkers do not understand how many of their other coworkers and supervisors can be so happy most of the time when things clearly are not going well. He also cannot figure out why he does not get higher ratings on his annual reviews and why he isn't selected for promotions. As you can see, Grant's negative thoughts and expectations have, in fact, become his reality.

Here is an example of the law of attraction working in a positive way with someone who has the mind of a champion:

Ryan has overcome many challenges in his life, from dealing with and mostly overcoming depression, anxiety, and the death of a close friend when he was a teenager. Through it all, however, Ryan has managed to learn coping skills to deal with his problems and, equally important, has learned to keep a positive attitude about his life and future. He stays away from negative people as much as possible. He has surrounded himself by like-minded positive people who share his enthusiasm and drive.

As an entrepreneur, he knows that he will face challenges at times, but he works hard, has a plan, and feels certain that things will work out, as they usually do. Ryan has managed to find a spouse with whom he is happy and who also has a positive and healthy attitude toward life. His colleagues, friends, and family members provide positivity, support, and encouragement, and, in turn, he provides the same for them. Ryan not only imagines what his life will ideally be like; he takes action to ensure that things in his life are the way he wants them to be, as does his spouse. He effectively utilizes the law of attraction in his life to create positive results.

Section IV: Time Keeps Moving Forward

One thing to remember as you strive to develop the mind of a champion is that, whether you like it or not, time keeps moving forward and will continue to do so. You are not getting any younger, nor is anyone else. Time does not wait for anyone. This means that your window of opportunity to develop the mind of a champion and to make your dreams and goals come to fruition is always diminishing. This does not mean that you should give up hope; it simply means that you should take advantage of the time you have and use it to your advantage. As long as you are in the mental and physical shape to be able to change your life, you can do so.

As an example of how you can develop your talents and passions, even if you are no longer in your youth, consider an artist named Anna Mary Robertson, more commonly known as Grandma Moses, born in 1860 in New York. She spent most of her life farming and serving as a wife and mother for her family. While she painted occasionally, she did not begin to devote much of her time and energy to creating her works of art, which often depicted rural settings, until she was into her seventies. Her artwork gained popularity, and she became an extremely famous artist, often creating new paintings and participating in exhibitions of her artwork. She also did not become an author until she was in her nineties, when she decided to write her autobiography. When she died at 101, she had devoted roughly thirty years of her life to her artwork.

Other people have devoted their lives to their passions, which they discovered at a much younger age. Some people began practicing sports when they were young. They kept practicing on a regular basis and improving their skills to become the best they could be, on and off the field. Other people have known since they were young that they were a natural educator; they developed that skill and devoted their lives to careers in education. All of these people took advantage of time and realized, in their own way, that time kept going.

Carpe diem is a common Latin saying. It means "seize the day." This concept has been written about extensively in literature, poems, novels, and works of nonfiction. The idea is that you never know how much time you have left on earth, so you should take advantage of the present, the now, the day that you have before you. People who live by this principle realize that there is no time like the present in which to fulfill their goals and make their ideal life come to fruition.

Realize that the concept of living life in the present does not go against the law of attraction, which emphasizes positive thinking. Positive thinking, surrounding yourself with positivity, and taking action are most definitely a way to make what you want to happen actually happen. The idea of seizing the day and of not knowing how much more time you have left is not a negative concept; it is entirely realistic.

The concept of carpe diem should spur you to go ahead and take action to make your ideal life happen and to get you further to reaching your goals and achieving your dreams. Instead of simply wishing all your life to become a successful ballerina, to write that book you've always wanted to create, to help those less fortunate than you, or to invent the next best umbrella, seize the opportunity you have right now and go for it. Don't wait thirty years to start working on making your dreams come true; do something constructive and concrete toward your goals now.

Seize the day! Instead of thinking about possibly doing something tomorrow, do it today. The sooner you take action that focuses on meeting your goals, the better. Time will never stop moving forward, so your focus should also be on moving forward so you can get where you want to go. If you think positively and seize the day, which may be your best—and maybe your only—opportunity, you may well reach your goals. Having goals is essential. You cannot, however, change the past or live in the future, so the present is what you have to work with. Make the best of now.

Section V: Raise Your Thinking and Your Standards

Raising your thinking as well as your standards is an integral part of your development in attaining the mind of a champion. All of this goes along with the concepts of knowing yourself, having a dedication to excellence, and utilizing the law of attraction. Raising your thinking can take many different forms, such as thinking in a more godly manner, thinking above and beyond how you can benefit from a situation to how you can help others as well, and thinking more like a person who is successful and has the mind of a champion rather than focusing on lower, more negative thoughts.

As the following Scripture shows, using God as a model can help you increase your standards and heighten your thinking:

> *I press toward the mark for the prize of the high calling of God in Christ Jesus. (Philippians 3:14)*

What is your measuring tool or marker? How do you figure out what your standards and level of thinking are? Do you measure yourself by looking at other people? We, as people, have a tendency to look at others and say or think that we are better than they are. We may look at other people and pat ourselves on the back because we do not make the mistakes that they have made or don't do what they do. We may even find ourselves wanting to spend time with people who have less or do less than us because that way we can feel better about ourselves. This is not the way to develop the mind of a champion.

If you, instead, raise your standards and change your environment so you are the little fish in a big pond, this affords you the opportunity to challenge yourself to improve, set new goals, and truly thrive and be successful. By challenging ourselves, we raise our standards and set ourselves up to gain new insight and success. Being out of your comfort zone encourages you to perform better and do things you may not have considered before because you did not have to.

Consider that you have to think higher to rise! Thinking higher will influence you to improve and to take your work or relationships, accomplishing greater things, to another level. Work on maturing and on raising your thinking and standards, and you will likely experience growth and positive results.

The following Scripture gives us excellent advice about raising our thinking and standards:

When I was a child, I spake as a child, I understood as a child, I thought as a child: but when I became a man, I put away childish things. (1 Corinthians 13:11)

This scripture teaches us that we must be mature in our speaking, understanding, and thinking. Simply being an adult is no guarantee that we are mature in the way we speak, understand, and think. This level of maturity is imperative when it comes to having a mind of a champion because we must remove childlike and immature ways from our lives.

For example, you will not always agree with someone, but how you speak and interact with that person demonstrates your maturity. Do you throw a temper tantrum when things don't work out according to your plan? Do you spend time pouting and not speaking to someone for whatever reason? Do you say whatever comes to mind and however you desire to say it? As an adult, you should no longer, as the Scripture says, speak, understand, or think like a child. You should have grown up and put away "childish things," such as immaturity, selfishness, or other self-defeating ways of thinking, reasoning, and acting. Your thinking and reasoning should be mature.

One way to raise your thinking and your standards is to work hard to increase your spirituality. As the next Scripture shows, focusing less on ourselves and more on God can definitely be beneficial:

He must increase, but I must decrease. (John 3:30)

We need more, not less, of God. The more presence He has in our lives, the better off we will be. God can live through us and manifest His fruit if we allow Him to. Of course, as we have mentioned before, besides the importance of your relationship with God, what you do, say, and think are directly related to your development of the mind of a champion. You need God in your life, but reaching your dreams and goals and having the right mindset will not happen without you taking action.

Here is an example of someone with lower-level thinking and standards:

Tim lives in an apartment in the same town where his family has always lived. He has been in and out of trouble for a number of offenses and, although he has learned from some of his mistakes, he has not turned his life around. At times he has had to depend on family and friends to get by, living with different people and having to ask for help with obtaining food and clothing. Sometimes he is able to hold a job and sometimes not, most recently working with a family friend on his construction crew. He would rather have others pay his bills while he spends time partying. He doesn't possess passion and zeal to become independent and self-sufficient, demonstrating a run-of-the-mill level of thinking and standards.

The following example, alternatively, is of a person with higher-level standards and thinking:

Sheila always wants to do her best. As a physician at a health clinic for low-income patients, she needs to, as her patients depend on her. She has worked hard to earn her medical degree and to become successful as a doctor. Her knowledge and analytical skills in various health issues is excellent, and her manner of interacting with patients, as well as coworkers, is exquisite. She only wants the best for her patients, she has helped lead the clinic to increasingly effective practices to benefit patients, and she always pushes herself to be her best. Her high standards and thinking are evident every day.

Next, in chapter 5, we examine two other factors in having the mind of a champion, determined focus and deliberate living.

Chapter 5:
Deliberate Living and Determined Focus

Section I: Living Life with Purpose and Intention

In this chapter, we will examine the important concepts of deliberate living and determined focus, both of which are central to developing the mind of a champion. This section of chapter 5 looks at living life with purpose and intention, as opposed to living haphazardly, without focus, goals, or deliberateness.

Before we get into discussing these concepts further, the Scripture below does an excellent job of summing up living with purpose:

> *You've all been to the stadium and seen the athletes race. Everyone runs; one wins. Run to win. All good athletes train hard. They do it for a gold medal that tarnishes and fades. You're after one that's gold eternally.*
>
> *I don't know about you, but I'm running hard for the finish line. I'm giving it everything I've got. No sloppy living for me! I'm staying alert and in top condition. I'm not going to get caught napping, telling everyone else all about it and then missing out myself. (1 Corinthians 9:24–27, MSG)*

As you can see here, living with purpose and intention means, among other things, to live with the right kinds of goals in mind and to do what you do purposefully, as opposed to haphazardly or without forethought. Not thinking ahead about what you do and acting impulsively can have negative consequences; living with purpose, on the other hand, can lead to extremely positive consequences and is a hallmark of a person who has the mind of a champion.

Living life with purpose means that you have goals. You have a reason to do the things you do. Having purpose gives you a reason to live, to work hard, and to succeed. Your purpose may come from your goals, from your desire to take care of your family, from your relationship with God, or from a combination of all of those factors. Discovering your real purpose in life, which may take some deep contemplation, is part of developing the mind of a champion. And the intense amount of effort it may take for you to discover your purpose and then to live your life with that purpose in mind is well worth the hard work it will require.

Living life with intention, the other part of this concept, means that you live and act intentionally and deliberately. You make decisions and then act on them based on your overall goals and dreams. You would not, for example, go to college and then choose your major because of what seemed interesting one random day or by drawing your major out of a hat. Doing that would go totally against the concept of living with intention. Choosing your major is something you should do deliberately, based on what your university offers, your purpose, innate abilities, interests, job market, and goals after college. Many people who want to become lawyers, for example, major in English or criminal justice.

In the same way, if one of your major goals is to lose weight and eat more nutritiously in order to become healthier, you would want to choose your foods, beverages, and exercise regimen with the intention of getting healthier, not randomly. So many people live their lives without purpose and intent, meaning they do not take the time to consider what they are doing and how what they are doing affects them now and can affect them in the future. Think about what you are doing, and align what you do with your goals and dreams.

When you live your life with purpose and intention, you set yourself on the path to developing the mind of a champion and to success. You should know what your purpose is and what your intentions are every morning when you wake up; this will keep you focused on your goals and on fulfilling your dreams. Remind yourself of your goals and dreams frequently so that working to fulfill them becomes a part of your everyday existence and your routine. In addition, strive to make decisions according to your purpose and destiny, not because everybody is doing it or because someone else wants you to.

Here is an example of someone living without purpose and intention:

Elliot has lived his life in an unremarkable way. He has always just gotten by and made it from one day to the next, never feeling like he had a strong and guiding purpose in his life. He has worked at the same job in the same company for several years, a job similar to the previous one he had at another company for several years before that. He has always been rather shiftless and aimless. Even though he does hold down a job and is married, though somewhat unhappily, he doesn't have a true purpose or intention to anchor his life. He isn't totally unhappy. He is just more in survival mode, making it from day to day without having any large goals in sight, except for his goal of retiring with a full retirement and Social Security at age sixty-five.

On the other hand, below is an example of someone living with purpose and intention:

Martha knows what she wants and how to go after it. She was always good at working with numbers and analyzing complex mathematical problems. In high school, she took Accounting I and Accounting II, and those classes ignited her purpose, so she decided to become an accountant. Thus, after high school, she applied to several universities that had excellent programs in accounting and was accepted into all of them. She chose the one that was her first choice and earned an academic scholarship.

After graduating from college with a degree in accounting, during which she took general business and management courses also, she became a certified public accountant (CPA) and went to work for a firm that specialized in corporate accounting. After several years of working there, she opened her own practice, which has been extremely successful.

Another of her life goals was to have a successful marriage and family. She became engaged to her husband while in college, and they married shortly after graduation. She and her husband work hard, instilling their values into their two children. Martha's priorities are her family and her career. She lives with purpose and intention, and the success she has experienced is evidence of that. Consequently, her life is thriving!

As you can see, living with purpose and intention makes it much more likely that you will succeed in reaching your goals, fulfilling your dreams, and being the best person you can possibly be.

Section II: Know Why You Do What You Do

Part of living in a way that demonstrates purpose and intention is knowing why you do what you do. In your life, everything you do should line up with your purpose, your calling, your destiny. If you have a definite goal or dreams but do things that do not help them to happen, then what you are doing is fruitless and likely a waste of your time and energy. Everything you do, once you have developed the mind of a champion, discovered your passions, and set your sights on your goals and dreams must lead to your dream in some way. If you do something but cannot explain why you are doing it, you may be wasting time and energy.

If you are going to enroll in a college degree program or take a professional development series of workshops, for example, you should have an idea of how this fits into your larger goals and dreams. Some may not be useful to your plans, or not aligned to your goals and dreams. If you want to work at a zoo, for instance, you may well want to take courses in biology, but a botany course, which would cover the study of plants instead of animals, wouldn't help you toward your goal. If your goal is to become a manager or supervisor at your workplace, for example, it would not make sense for you to become frequently involved in confrontations with your coworkers or supervisors or to be lazy in your work. Knowing why you are doing what you are doing and paying attention to the details is necessary for success.

If your goal is to become a better communicator with members of your family, friends, and coworkers, think carefully about what you need to do. You could spend the rest of your life, literally, reading all the books and websites you could find about improving your communication; however, this would be a waste of your time and energy since you would not have a chance to implement any of what you read about. Instead, a better approach, and one that would be utilized by someone with the mind of a champion, would be to choose two or three sources of information about communication skills. Then read those carefully and work hard to test out and implement some of the strategies in your life. You would want to take a critical look at your own deficits in communication, so you can improve them, and build on your communication strengths. You could then more carefully select what to read or study about communication skills. Likewise, if you want to become a better communicator at work, it would behoove you to observe and even ask advice from someone there who has effective communication skills.

In whatever you pursue, your reason has to be compelling, motivating, and firm for you to continue to pursue your dreams or goals. If your "why" is not firm and fixed in your mind, then the least bit of challenge or trouble will cause you to quit. There was a single mother who wanted to set an example for her children while better positioning herself for a career as opposed to her current job. Her children became her "why." When times became challenging, when she was balancing work, school, and parenting responsibilities, she would always go back to "why" she was pursuing her college degree. Her "why" was the driving force to push her through the difficult days and long nights of studying for exams and completing assignments.

What is your "why" as you pursue your goals and dreams? If your "why" does not push you past challenges and the pain of disappointment and setbacks, then you have to reexamine why you are pursuing your goal or aspiration.

Next we will look at an effective way to make sure you know what you are doing, which is developing a road map.

Section III: A Road Map to Your Destiny

Each morning when you wake up, you should know where you are going. You should also know how you will get there. In other words, you should know what you are going to do and how you are going to do it. That does not mean that your journey will always be simple, easy to predict, and free from challenges. What it does mean is that you are able to handle bumps in the road, challenges, or obstacles as they arise.

You need a road map that will help guide you to your ultimate goals. You must map out a strategy or plan to get you where you desire to be. Life is calling you. To get to where you need to be in life, you need a plan, or a road map. Ideally, you will have a plan as well as backup plans.

What is a road map? Similar to a physical map or a global positioning system (GPS), a road map is a guide that tells you how to get somewhere. It tells you, from where you are starting out, what places to go through, what turns to make, and other useful information, such as distance (usually in miles) between places. Some modern GPS systems also give information, such as obstacles that you should be on the lookout for. A figurative road map would serve the same purpose; it would tell a person what they need to do to reach a destination. In this case, however, the road map needs to be written by the person making the journey.

If you are creating the road map based on your goals, you might have everything you need to do in your mind and not need to write it down. Or you might decide to write down everything in the format of a narrative or a spreadsheet. In any case, you could write down various things to create your road map.

Keep in mind: What is your ultimate goal? What are the individual steps you need to take in order to get there? When do you want to have each step, or subgoal, completed? What will you need to do to get each step completed? What obstacles do you have to look out for, and what can you do to overcome each obstacle? What supplies and resources do you need to complete each step and to reach your overall goal? Who can help you reach your goals, and how? Think about and decide on all of these factors as you create your road map. Realize, of course, that some of your goals and strategies, parts of your road map, can change along the way even if your larger goal remains the same.

What might a road map look like? First and foremost, every person's road map will look fairly different since each person has individual goals and dreams. A road map for someone wanting to overcome an addiction and be a good spouse and parent would look much different from one for someone wanting to become an expert electrician, for example. The road map you create on the way to reaching your goals and fulfilling your dreams is highly individualized and unique. What it does is to ensure that you have a plan to reach your goals.

You road map must, of course, be somewhat flexible since circumstances change, you may fail at one part of your plan and have to try something different, you may have multiple ideas about how to reach smaller goals or your big goal, and you may run into an unexpected opportunity that helps get you closer to your ultimate goal. Revise your road map, as changes occur. Flexibility and an ability to make adjustments are a hallmark of having the mind of a champion. Accept that life is generally unpredictable as you develop your road map and goals.

Following is an example of a person utilizing a road map to get where he wants to go and fulfill his goals:

Thomas has always wanted to go into politics, as he believes that serving his fellow man is an honorable goal. In high school, he takes classes in speech and debate to learn as much as he can about American and world history. He also takes advantage of his English courses to learn better written and oral communication skills, as well as analytical skills. In addition, he learns about statistics from his courses. He knows that he wants to go to college and probably major in political science. After graduating from high school, attending the college of his choice, and majoring in political science, he plans the next steps on his road map.

While in college, he makes friends as well as useful connections with classmates, political science professors, and acquaintances he meets through his field work and membership in campus political organizations. He assists with the political campaign of a woman running for reelection for the House of Representatives in his state and with the campaign of a man running for the U.S. Senate.

Once he graduates from college, he goes to work full time as an assistant to a state senator and then continues making connections and planning, looking carefully for an opportune time to start his own run for state senate. After one unsuccessful run for state senate, he runs again and is elected, beginning his political career. As conditions in the political landscape change, so does his road map. All the while, however, Thomas is utilizing a road map to reach his goals.

Section IV: Deliberate Living: Planting the Right Seeds

Deliberate living is consistently planting the right seeds. To use a farming analogy, if your goal is to grow corn to sell and to feed your family, planting squash, tomato, or onion seeds would not be an effective use of your time. None of these would produce the corn you are looking for. Deliberate living means taking the right steps, or planting the right seeds, to make your goals come true, ones that you have thought carefully about, ones that fit into your larger goals, and ones that go along with your road map.

Deliberate living and planting the right seeds also refers to maintaining a strong focus on your goals, a vitally important element in developing the mind of a champion. Deliberate living is having immense focus and attention on each seed you plant in accomplishing your dreams and goals. You are intentional in that you plant seeds that will certainly produce the harvest of your dream. You can't expect to achieve anything if you have not put the time and effort toward a particular goal. You must put the work in and be disciplined throughout the process before you reap the benefit. Many people desire to achieve greatness, but they are not willing to spend the time it takes or are not as disciplined as they need to be.

Dreams and goals do not simply happen. It is easy to dream about what you want your life to be like or about being successful, but you must take action to make things happen. It takes deliberately putting all your energy, effort, resources, and mind toward accomplishing those dreams and goals. Olympic athletes are deliberate in their quest for competing and earning a gold medal; they go through daily rigorous training for hours, are disciplined in what they eat, and rest adequately to maximize their performance. The Olympic athlete rises early in the morning to go for a long run or hit the weight room and then returns later in the evening to swim more laps in the pool. For four years the Olympic athlete harnesses his emotions and disciplines himself to a lifestyle of deliberate living. It is this approach you must take if you desire to accomplish greatness with your dreams and goals. Thus I urge you to focus and be deliberate about everything you do, as greatness awaits you!

Here is an example of people who have not planted the right seeds:

Steven and Heather, when raising their two children, decided to forgo the process of teaching their children respect, discipline, and effective communication. Steven and Heather would never correct the children's inappropriate behavior, and they allowed the children to do as they pleased. They figured correcting the children's behavior was no big deal. Now, however, those seeds are truly evident. David, age thirteen, and Mary, age sixteen, are argumentative, disobedient, and disrespectful to their parents and school administrators.

Steven and Heather cannot easily go back, dig up the seeds they planted, and plant new seeds now that their children are teenagers. Therefore, they must deal with the consequences of allowing their children to do as they pleased and planting the wrong seeds. Unfortunately, their son and daughter suffer because of their parents' negligence and haphazard seed planting. (This does not mean, however, that at some point David and Mary could not turn things around by their own wise choices in their lives; they could.)

Alternatively, here is an example of a person who has planted the right seeds:

Janice has made it a goal of hers to have inner peace as well as peace with those around her. As she worked to get centered, she found that participating in meditation, Bible study and worship at church, therapy, and exercise helped her to feel calm. As a young adult, she suffered some from anxiety and had some difficulty in relating to people. Once she found the techniques that worked for her, Janice learned how to implement them into her daily routine as much as possible or as needed. She also worked to maintain peace, balance, and harmony in her relationships with those around her, such as family, including her husband and daughter, friends, other churchgoers, and coworkers. She has worked hard to demonstrate respect for other people, and that respect is most often reciprocated back to her. At work, she has excellent relationships with her workers, who respect her, enjoy her being part of the team, and value her opinion.

Janice and her husband have planted the seeds of discipline, loving parenting, nurturing respect, love, and empathy in their children, who have developed these qualities and made them part of their underlying character. Her children also know that they can always tell her anything they need to and that they can come to her and their father for advice. Janice and her husband have demonstrated and emphasized the importance of quality family time. Planting the right seeds in this case has made Janice an excellent mother and a positive influence on her children. The work she puts into relationships—the figurative seeds that she plants—makes all the difference.

Section V: Determined Focus: Exercising Self-discipline

One essential aspect of keeping a determined focus is self-discipline. Self-discipline refers to the ability to keep yourself under control, doing what you need to and are supposed to be doing at the time you should be doing it, despite distractions, temptations, or personal weaknesses. Self-discipline means having an ability to exercise self-control. Having self-discipline also means that you can control your impulses and remain steadily focused on the tasks at hand.

For example, I routinely work out three to four times a week, but each day is new day that I am faced with the choice to work out or not; some days it takes nothing for me to get out of bed, but other days I have to truly exhibit the mind of a champion by resisting the emotions and desire to stay put. Even if the work you are trying to do feels challenging, boring, or redundant, as it will sometimes, exercising self-discipline means that you are able to keep going and finish your tasks so that you can reach your dreams and fulfill your goals; this is another hallmark of having or developing the mind of a champion.

The following Scripture relates to the concept of self-discipline:

> *And every man that striveth for the mastery is temperate in all things. Now they do it to obtain a corruptible crown; but we an incorruptible. (1 Corinthians 9:25)*

As you can see from the Scripture above, the Bible alludes to the importance of self-discipline, or of being temperate in what you do. If you are temperate, you show self-restraint or moderation.

You stand to gain many benefits from exercising self-discipline. Self-discipline will help you stay on track with your goals and plans. It will help you utilize your road map effectively. It will help you to continually make progress. If you have had difficulty in the past maintaining self-discipline, which is common, you may find that you have to work harder than the average person to develop your own unique methods of self-discipline; however, you will find in the end that consistent self-discipline is a great way to reach your goals and fulfill your dreams.

There are various reasons people have difficulty with self-discipline include lack of motivation, impatience, and a lack of stick-to-itiveness. A lack of self-discipline could also be due to medical or mental health reasons; get tested if you suspect you have a physical problem. A lack of self-discipline is a major roadblock that keeps people from success.

A person lacking self-discipline may never fulfill their dreams and goals. They may dream big but make little progress toward goals, leading to persistent frustration.

Here is an example of someone who does not exercise self-discipline:

Gary has dreamed all his life of becoming an author. He has always been an avid reader, although he does not always finish reading the books he starts. Gary works as a loan officer at a credit union, which is not his passion, so his job is rather unsatisfying, but he has to pay the bills. He has no trouble coming up with topics he wants to write about; often as he is supposed to be working he is instead jotting down ideas for short stories, novels, or nonfiction books or articles he would like to write. However, nothing much ever happens with these ideas. He went to a writer's workshop once, a few years ago, and planned to spend time writing every day. However, that was ten years ago, and his plan of writing regularly never materialized.

On the other hand, here is example of someone who does exercise self-discipline:

Tyrone is an award-winning author. He spends three to four hours writing every single day, no matter how he feels. He has kept this up for several years and is convinced that this simple exercise in self-discipline is what helps him to succeed. It takes a great deal of time, effort, and consistency for Tyrone to be able to write like he does, but he is convinced that it is worth it, as are his readers.

In the next chapter, chapter 6, we will look at the importance of taking opportunities when they come and seizing the moment. We have discussed this earlier, but now, considering the importance of this concept, we will examine it in greater detail.

Chapter 6:
Seize the Moment: Window of Opportunity

Section I: Tomorrow

Seizing the moment is vitally important in the process of developing the mind of a champion and of being successful. Taking advantage of the window of opportunity that you have is crucial to success. Before we go into depth about that, let us discuss the opposite of taking advantage of windows of opportunity: procrastination. Instead of taking initiative now or taking advantage of some opportunity that has come our way, many of us decide to wait until later. We decide that we should do whatever it is tomorrow instead of now!

In the following Scripture, the concept of tomorrow is important:

> *Then Pharaoh called for Moses and Aaron, and said, Intreat the LORD, that he may take away the frogs from me, and from my people; and I will let the people go, that they may do sacrifice unto the LORD. And Moses said unto Pharaoh, Glory over me: when shall I intreat for thee, and for thy servants, and for thy people, to destroy the frogs from thee and thy houses, that they may remain in the river only?*

And he said, Tomorrow. And he said, Be it according to thy word: that thou mayest know that there is none like unto the LORD our God. (Exodus 8:8–10)

We wonder, after reading this, why Pharaoh did not decide that the frogs, which were part of a plague and causing problems, should be gotten rid of immediately instead of tomorrow. Clearly "now" would have been a much more satisfactory answer than "tomorrow."

We should seize every moment and every opportunity available that will help us reach our goals. What we should say is "today" instead of "tomorrow."

Following are some of the things that people have a habit of waiting to do, of saying "tomorrow" about:

- Tomorrow I'll lose weight/eat right/exercise: If one of your goals is to get healthier, then the best time to start is today. Don't wait until tomorrow. This is one of those goals that people often set as one of their New Year's resolutions and then promptly ignore. If you really mean it, then start now. The more you get in the habit of living healthier, the easier it is to keep living healthily.
- Tomorrow I'll start school: People often decide to wait until later to start some type of educational program. It could be working on getting a GED (high school diploma) for someone who never graduated. It could be going to college. Or it could be starting some type of job training or professional development to gain more skills. If educational opportunities are important to reaching your goals, then putting off schooling may well

keep you from being successful and developing the mind of a champion.

- Tomorrow I'll start to save: Financially, you are almost always better off, if at all possible, to start to save now rather than waiting. Saving money for the future or for emergencies is important, so the sooner the better.
- Tomorrow I'll look for a job: If you decide to wait until tomorrow to look for a job, whether you just need a job or are looking for your dream job, you will likely miss out. If you, for example, keep waiting because you only want the perfect job, then you may be waiting the rest of your life. Having some job that starts you toward your goals, or that at least helps pay the bills, is better than having no job at all. As the old saying goes, "The early bird catches the worm."
- Tomorrow I'll start going to church: This is what people say when they face life's problems and challenges. People have a tendency to attend church or pray when they are in a difficult situation; however, God desires a personal relationship with us. A personal relationship means we spend time in corporate worship and private devotion daily. Thus putting church off until tomorrow (next Sunday) is denying your soul the spiritual nutriment it needs to live a fruitful life.

Why do we say tomorrow? This bad habit keeps us from fulfilling our goals and being the best we can be. Realize that when you say you'll do something tomorrow, when tomorrow comes you tend to again say "tomorrow." Tomorrow may never turn into today.

Procrastinators put off until tomorrow what they could do today. And the bottom line for procrastinators is this: you will miss many opportunities to make things happen in your life. When you continually put things off and don't take advantage of opportunities as they come along and don't take action that could help, you are not displaying the mind of a champion.

The below Scripture addresses the concept of procrastination, or of sleeping through opportunities:

> *How long wilt thou sleep, O sluggard? when wilt thou arise out of thy sleep? (Proverbs 6:9)*

As is clear from this proverb, procrastinating, putting everything off until tomorrow, is the equivalent of sleeping your life away and failing to take advantage of the here and now that is available to you.

In the next section, we will look at one big reason that people procrastinate. The fear of failure often holds people back so they wait instead of acting when they should.

Section II: Fear of Failure

One major reason many people do not take advantage of the moment is a fear of failure. People sometimes think that if they don't try something in the first place, they cannot fail at it. They think if they put in no effort at all, they can't fail. Lack of trying, however, is a type of failure.

Some people might be afraid, for example, to go into business for themselves because they think they will fail and are not capable; they are too afraid to do it, so they do nothing instead. Doing nothing is, of course, simply another form of fear of failure, as is trying and coming up short of the goal. If you have the mind of a champion, you will not let being afraid of failure stop you from trying to reach your goals.

According to this Scripture, God does not want us to be afraid:

For God hath not given us the spirit of fear; but of power, and of love, and of a sound mind. (2 Timothy 1:7)

Instead, He wants us to know that we have, besides a sound mind, a spirit of love and of power. It is up to us whether we utilize these or not. God has designed people to be strong and courageous. Utilize the love, strength, rationality, power, and courage that God has bestowed upon you to reach your goals. Take advantage of what God has given you and use it. He gave you talents, abilities, and the ability to be powerful and rational for a reason. Show your appreciation for what He has given you by utilizing your gifts!

Keep in mind that doing nothing because of your fear of failure does not teach you much. At least if you try something and fail at it, you can learn from the failure and try to prevent a similar occurrence in the future. The truth is that most people who are successful and who have the mind of a champion have not always reached their goals on the first or second attempt. Through failing, they learn to be more successful in the future.

Some authors, for example, have to face rejection for their work dozens or even hundreds of times. They may send a book manuscript to one hundred publishers to see if the company will publish it and may be rejected each time. Instead of giving up, these writers are persistent and do not give up simply because they have "come up short" one or more times. Fear of failure does not help anyone. Some things in life are sensible to fear, such as being scared to jump unprotected from a high distance; that fear makes sense and can save your life. A fear of failure, however, will not serve any useful purpose and should not be a characteristic of a person who has developed the mind of a champion. A level of fear and anxiety is normal and expected when you step out of your comfort zone, but it must not paralyze you to the point where you do nothing.

For example, I desired to obtain a doctoral degree, and when I entered the program I was excited. However, I experienced some fear and anxiety in terms of my ability to accomplish such a high and lofty goal. Yet, even with my fear and anxiety, I continued to move forward, refusing to be paralyzed, and was able to accomplish my goal.

On the other hand, your goals should be realistic and obtainable. If your only goal is to become the conductor of a *particular* orchestra, you have only a small chance to obtain that position, no matter how talented you are. This goal, in other words, is not easily obtainable. You might want to pursue a goal of becoming a conductor of *any* orchestra instead of a specific one. Likewise, if your only goal is to make a living as a professional hockey player, this may or may not become a reality since so few people make it. Since this goal may not become a reality or if you become a professional hockey player you will not play hockey forever, then you should have another goal to achieve while you keep practicing hockey.

Imagine you have lived your whole life with a deep sense of fear of being unsuccessful. You may have had many different goals. Maybe you wanted to have a happy marriage with the right person. Maybe you wanted to open your own construction company or hair salon. Even though you had these dreams and goals, your phobia kept you from pursuing them; you weren't able to get past these fears. In the end, you were too afraid of being rejected in a relationship or of not being successful in running your own business. Instead, you settled and never did pursue your dreams. You definitely did not develop the mind of a champion.

Imagine how many regrets you will have if you never bother to pursue your dreams because of your fear of failure. Instead, make a conscious choice to pursue your dreams and goals, even if that means that you may risk failing at times, which it does. Going for your dreams means taking risks. While it may sometimes be easier and seem safer simply to settle for what you have now, if you are truly passionate about your dreams, you will decide that the risks are worth it and go for it. If you go for your dreams, you will likely feel exhilarated and extremely proud of what you accomplish, from the small steps along the way to the large successes you eventually will experience.

Don't let opportunities pass you by!

Section III: Seize the Moment

Let us again discuss the concept of seizing the moment, this time in more detail. This concept is so important to the development of the mind of a champion and to fulfilling your goals and dreams that we need to emphasize it again.

Benjamin Franklin, a historical American figure, said: "You may delay, but time will not." What does this mean? It means that while you may decide to set aside your goals, time will keep on passing. You will not get younger. You will not get to go back and change any decisions you made in the past or take advantage of any opportunities you missed. Time will move ahead whether you want to or not. Since all that you are guaranteed is the present, take advantage of opportunities that come your way.

It is easy to let opportunities pass you by, which means that you are not seizing the moment. On the other hand, you should not take every opportunity that comes your way because some are not advisable. If you were given the chance to work your dream job but in a place that had terrible management, low employee morale, salary too low to pay your living expenses, and a consistently negative reputation, then you should most likely pass on that opportunity and look for better ones. But if a chance comes along that will help you reach your goals and fulfill your dreams, then seize the moment and go for it.

Remember this: God wants you to seize the moment. He wants you to take the right opportunity to step out of your comfort zone. If you are afraid to step out of your comfort zone, you may well miss important chances that come your way.

When seizing the moment, do not be persuaded by people who are not interested in your best interests or in you reaching your God-given destiny. You may have to step away from the noise of negative people and surround yourself with those who are like minded and aligned with your value system. Step out from the crowd and up to the plate. Each person in life will get unique opportunities; each individual must make the decision whether to seize them or not.

It is easy to be like everyone else and blend in with the crowd, but this will not get you far in life. To truly develop the mind of a champion and to reach your goals, you need to not only know yourself and be comfortable with yourself but let your individuality and talents shine through. Shining as an individual includes seizing the moment when great opportunities present themselves.

Think about this: every year thousands of people graduate from college. This is great and is a major accomplishment, but if you want to excel in your field, you will need to do something to differentiate yourself from everyone else competing for the same opportunities. If your degree is in fashion design and you want to make a name for yourself in that field, you might apply for and take an internship with a well-known fashion designer to make yourself stand out.

You might have to move across the country or even to another country take advantage of an opportunity that comes your way.

When a good opportunity comes along, seriously consider taking advantage of it; you never know when or if another opportunity will ever come your way again. You don't want to let low self-esteem or fear of failure get in the way of a wonderful chance you could take advantage of.

Consider this example of a person seizing the moment:

Tracy grew up in a household with loving parents, money, and plenty of opportunities. She went to college, as she and her parents had planned, but she got into trouble and made bad decisions along the way. Around the time she was a sophomore in college, she continued to make bad decisions, hung out with the wrong people, and became heavily involved in various types of mind-altering and addictive drugs. She ended up dropping out of college, having children, having her children taken away from her due to her drug use, working menial jobs that were not satisfying, and going from relationship to relationship. Years later, when she finally got off drugs, got her children back, and got her life in order, she was able to finish her college degree. Still, however, she did not seem to have many career opportunities open to her.

One day the opportunity came along for a temporary sales job. Tracy took this opportunity, worked hard, and ended up turning this chance opportunity into a full-time career that she stayed with for years. She discovered that her socialization and persuasion skills helped her to succeed in the world of sales. Had she not seized the moment and taken the job, giving it her all, who knows what would've happened in her life?

Seizing the moment is great, but if you aren't the best that you can be, you may still hold yourself back. We will examine this important concept next.

Section IV: Be the Best You Can Be

Consider this Bible verse about Jesus's disciple Peter:

> *And in the fourth watch of the night Jesus went unto them, walking on the sea. And when the disciples saw him walking on the sea, they were troubled, saying, It is a spirit; and they cried out for fear. But straightway Jesus spake unto them, saying, Be of good cheer; it is I; be not afraid. And Peter answered him and said, Lord, if it be thou, bid me come unto thee on the water. And he said, Come. And when Peter was come down out of the ship, he walked on the water, to go to Jesus. But when he saw the wind boisterous, he was afraid; and beginning to sink, he cried, saying, Lord, save me. And immediately Jesus stretched forth his hand, and caught him, and said unto him, O thou of little faith, wherefore didst thou doubt? (Matthew 14:25–31)*

Even though he was somewhat afraid, Peter was the only disciple who walked on water. He took a chance, seized the moment, and showed what he was truly capable of. You could be like Peter, taking chances and, even if you have some fear, doing what needs to be done. Peter was the best he could be for his Lord Jesus Christ.

In developing the mind of a champion, you that must be the best you can be. If you aren't your best, then you can't expect to go as far as you may want to. Being the best requires motivation, energy, focus, and determination. It is much easier to perform at a mediocre level; however, this type of tepid performance will likely not impress anyone.

Following is an example of a group of people not being the best they can be:

At a fast food restaurant in a small town, a team of cooks, cashiers, drive-through workers, and managers makes it through every day, but since most of them are not trying to be the best they can be, no one is truly impressed with their food or customer service. Most everything about this restaurant and its workers can be described as mediocre. The restaurant makes money, but think how much more money it could make and how much more satisfaction it could provide to its employees if everyone truly worked at their highest capacity. In fact, to see what everyone is truly capable of you would need to watch this group in action when the district manager is there or when corporate executives visit. At times like these, everyone works as hard as he or she is capable of. It is amazing what a little pressure can make people do.

How do you know that you are being the best you can be? When you are using all of your abilities and demonstrating peak performance. Of course, everyone has different ability levels, but people are often amazed at what they are truly capable of. If you want to be the best singer, you may have to practice frequently, expand your range of genres and song types, and learn many songs and/or write your own songs.

If you want to be a successful writer, you may be able to learn something from the methods that best-selling author Stephen King has used. King began writing as a teenager. He earned a bachelor's degree in English, which was a good start, and then he honed his craft. In addition to reading thousands of books, he has developed a routine where he writes a set number of words, if not more, every workday. Besides being critical of his own work, King turns over his manuscripts to his harshest critic, his wife; she gives him an honest and unvarnished opinion about the quality, or lack thereof, of his work. King polishes his manuscripts, showing that he is working to be the best writer he can be. The key to being the greatest in your chosen field is to master your craft!

As you have hopefully been doing throughout this book, consider what your goals are and what you need to do to continue developing the mind of a champion. Are you now the best you can be? If not, what do you need to do to improve? Do you demonstrate the drive and determination to push yourself to consistently be your best? If not, what can you do to start improving the quality of your performance? These questions are relevant for whatever goal you have, whether you are trying to begin a new career, improve your relationships, etc.

Being the best you can may look different for different people, depending on their individual goals. If you want to be a star football player, then you will need to work out strenuously, practice football consistently, be the best teammate you can, learn from your mistakes, and improve on your successes. If you want to improve your interpersonal relationships with family, you will likewise have several things to do to be your best; these could include seeing a therapist, working hard every day to get along with your family, taking care of your family, taking care of yourself, and being honest in assessing your personal strengths and weaknesses. There is no shortcut to being your best. Consistent hard work and striving to excel and push yourself to improve are what it takes to be the best you can be. And if you are putting forth your best effort on a continual basis, this should make you feel good and can definitely help to improve your self-esteem. This is all part of developing the mind of a champion.

Section V: Window of Opportunity

First, let's establish exactly what a window of opportunity is, since this somewhat figurative phrase could be easily misinterpreted. A window of opportunity is a critical period during which you either seize an opportunity or it could be lost. Such is the critical importance of taking opportunities as they come that we are again examining a concept that is closely related. If you have the mind of a champion, you will seize every desirable moment and every opportunity as it becomes available to you. The key to the window of opportunity is timing, life situations, and the power of investment.

Let's look at a couple examples of this concept.

Jessica is an administrative assistant with a small firm. She has been there a few years and is highly successful in her work. Some of the positive aspects of her job are that she gets to be where the action is and has a moderate level of responsibility over several areas, all of which are going well for her. A couple of negatives are that she has begun to feel that she needs to move on to a better opportunity and that she is not paid as highly as she thinks she ought to be, based on her level of responsibility and her research comparing salaries for administrative assistants.

One day she hears from a colleague about an opening for an administrative assistant at a larger company. She finds out as many details as she can from her colleague and then inquires about the position, including reading the position description. Jessica realizes that she has all of the required skills and experiences needed for the position. She also realizes that the new job would give her a higher level of responsibility, more autonomy over her work, and much higher pay. However, she has been in her current position for seven years and, even though she knows she wants more, is somewhat hesitant to leave. Plus, what if she applies for it and doesn't get it? That would make her feel bad. She spends weeks waffling, going back and forth, trying to decide if she should apply or not. Finally, she decides that she will apply and take her chances.

When she goes online to apply, however, she learns that the position is no longer available and has already been filled; her colleague who told her about the possibility confirms this. Would Jessica have moved up to a better position with higher pay and more responsibility? She will never know because she neglected to seize the moment; she did not move while the window of opportunity was available. Maybe next time something like that comes open, she will go for it!

Consider this example also:

Stephanie is a business major in college. She has worked hard and is in her junior year. She has taken all the required classes, including foreign language, which for her, based on her plans in international business, was Italian. Because of the lack of organization within her academic department, opportunities to study abroad have been extremely limited. This experience, while definitely helpful, is not a requirement for graduation. One day as she is meeting with her advisor to do a degree audit, he mentions an opportunity to study abroad for a semester in Italy. The deadline for application, however, is only a few days away.

Stephanie decides that this opportunity would be an excellent experience for her. Right away, she talks to her department head. While she learns that she will probably have to spend one more semester in college in order to graduate if she goes to study abroad for a semester, she agrees the opportunity would be worth it. Stephanie discusses the opportunity with her parents, who agree that she should study abroad in Italy.

She then thoroughly but quickly completes the online application, including procuring the two required faculty references. Two weeks later, she is approved to study abroad. She has a valuable experience in the study and application of international business principles in Italy. When she begins her career, she credits this opportunity as being extremely valuable. Had Stephanie not taken advantage of this very short window of opportunity, either because she was indecisive or waited too long to complete the application process, she would have missed out.

As you can see, windows of opportunity exist only for a finite amount of time. When a window closes, if that opportunity comes around again, it will not present itself as it did before. For example, I encourage young people to obtain all of their education before they get too engrossed in their career or life. I share with them that continuing on in school to achieve a master's degree immediately after achieving a bachelor's degree, or at least within one or two years of the bachelor's degree, provides a window of opportunity that will be different if they wait to pursue it until later in life. By this time, the student could be married with kids as opposed to being a single adult.

Enrolling in college at the age of forty to obtain a bachelor's degree is a window of opportunity as well for the person who dropped out of college to care for an ill parent or child or who simply had "life happen." If you do not seize the moment, the window of opportunity presented to you in the future could change. A window of opportunity is also about making the right investment at the right time, one that will yield you a greater dividend in the future. It's when you decide to invest time to study and prepare to become a master brain surgeon, it's when you invest time to go to seminary to learn how to study the Bible. On the other hand, if you don't attend seminary, you still take the time to study and pray in preparing your sermons. You invest time to write articles and submit to a magazine for publication in preparing to become an author. You enroll in college and prepare to become a schoolteacher. All of these are examples of investing to achieve your goal. Only commit your time and financial resources to windows of opportunities that align with your purpose and that will lead to you accomplishing your dreams and goals.

Having the foresight to realize when a window of opportunity may be valuable to your pursuit of your goals and dreams is an important ability of one who truly has the mind of a champion. One who does not seize the moment will find closed windows of opportunity and, possibly, closed doors in the future. Don't let excellent opportunities pass you by. Someone else will take advantage of them if you do not!

Next, in the final chapter of this book, we will look at the importance of what you say and how you say it.

Chapter 7:

It's How You Speak: Free Yourself

Section I: Words Can Hurt or Help You

An old saying goes like this: "Sticks and stones can break my bones, but words can never hurt me." The truth is, however, as most of us know, that words can hurt; alternatively, words can help.

The words you use go along with what is in your mind and with the actions you take (or do not take). Earlier we discussed the importance of thinking positive thoughts and messages. Here we will examine the significance of the words you use in conversation with other people.

Look at the following Scripture regarding words and their power:

Death and life are in the power of the tongue: and they that love it shall eat the fruit thereof. (Proverbs 18:21)

Words are not only vital, but they can be the difference between life and death. And those who use words correctly will benefit from doing so.

Words can be used in many ways both to help or hurt other people or yourself. Imagine, for example, that you went to a job interview for a position in which you were truly interested. If you were asked how you usually performed at one of the important tasks required for the job, you could say, "I'm okay at it, I guess." The problem with this response is that, while it may come natural to some people, it is not beneficial for a job interview. It sounds as if you are lacking self-confidence, are not good at that particular skill, or both. The response could also make you sound somewhat dishonest, as if you're trying to cover for the fact that you lack skills in a certain area.

Here is how words could be used to help in the same situation:

Brenda is asked in a job interview—for the position of drug store assistant manager—how she usually is at dealing with difficult customers. She replies in a way that is confident but humble, saying, "Since I have retail experience and have dealt with many different types of customers, from pleasant to downright rude, I find that I am able to interact effectively with all types of customers, even the difficult ones." This sounds much more confident than the previous response of, "I'm okay at it, I guess," without sounding arrogant.

Other examples of words being used in a way that is harmful in professional relationships includes being rude to colleagues, arguing for no good reason with coworkers, dismissing the ideas of coworkers, and criticizing colleagues for no reason.

Words are also important in relationships with family and friends. In these relationships, words can also help or hurt you or other people.

Here is an example of words being used in a hurtful way in a family relationship:

Scott and his wife Teri sometimes disagree, which is normal for married couples. Both Scott and Teri, however, seem to have a problem with their tempers. When they disagree, their tempers sometimes flare, so harmful words come out of their mouths. In the heat of an argument, they both have the tendency to use profanity with each other or to call each other names, none of which lend anything constructive to their discussions. Instead of making things calmer or helping them to reach any conclusions, this misuse of words simply escalates the disagreement, increasing their anger toward one another and making it harder for them to make up and move on. They have been known, for example, to make insulting remarks about each other's weight, intelligence, or looks.

Here, on the other hand, is an example of words being used in a helpful and beneficial way in a family situation:

Bob and his wife Heather sometimes disagree, but when they do, they do not let their arguments get too far out of hand. Usually, though not 100% of the time, they listen respectfully to one another's opinions and state in a calm manner how they disagree and why they think the other person's opinion or idea is incorrect or could be improved. Neither one resorts to calling each other names, personally insulting the other, or using profanity when they argue because they know that nothing good comes out of that kind of interaction. Because of their mutual respect for one another, they both feel free to say what they think to one another and express their thoughts and feelings freely.

Heather and Bob are also not hesitant to be assertive with one another when they feel that they need to be, but they still do this in a respectful manner. They know how to take up for themselves and how to do so in a constructive manner. Bob and Heather seem to make a great deal more progress in their relationship than do Teri and Scott, who perhaps one day will learn the importance and power of words. As Proverbs 15:1 says: "A soft answer turneth away wrath: but grievous words stir up anger." It is within our ability to speak in a way that edifies and is not harmful, starting with our voice tone!

Overall, keep in mind that words have great power; words matter as much as actions. Evaluate people based on both their words and actions. People who speak softly and kindly but quietly do things to harm other people are as bad as people who speak loudly and meanly to others. The bottom line is that words matter.

Section II: You Are What You Say

Think of this principle: You are what you say. There are several ways to consider this concept. If you want to be free and liberated from a past situation, then you must believe in your heart and speak that you are free from it. If you want to be set free, speak that you are free. If you want to be a winner, say that you are a winner. If you want to live, then speak life into your soul. If you want to be healed, speak about your healing.

In life, you must learn that what you speak is a reflection of your mindset. Unless you are dishonest, then what you say reveals what you think and believe. Your mindset shows in what you say about yourself and about your ability to accomplish something.

Stop the habit of using words against yourself. People use words against themselves in many ways, including insulting themselves or calling themselves names. Instead, build yourself up. Remember that if you talk about yourself in a negative way, other people are likely to do the same. Use words to acknowledge your talents and strengths. Talking in a positive manner about the work you have done when discussing your progress with your supervisor or with a client in a business situation will help you to feel good about what you've done and will help your supervisor or client to see the value in and good things about your work.

Consider the Scripture below.

And David's two wives were taken captives, Ahinoam the Jezreelitess, and Abigail the wife of Nabal the Carmelite. And David was greatly distressed; for the people spake of stoning him, because the soul of all the people was grieved, every man for his sons and for his daughters: but David encouraged himself in the LORD his God. (1 Samuel 30:5–6)

In this Scripture, David encouraged himself. He used his strong faith in God as a way to encourage and strengthen himself in the Lord. David used words, whether he spoke them aloud or in his mind, to give himself the strength and the courage to handle this extremely scary and discouraging situation, where people spoke of stoning him to death. If David can use words to get himself in the right mindset in such a serious life-or-death situation, then we should also be able to use words to help us. David was courageous in the face of a deadly threat. Therefore, we are what we say.

If nobody loves you, for example, then love yourself first. You must learn to look yourself in the mirror and find your strength and power in God; at the same time, you must also find strength within to handle any challenges that come your way and to speak in a way that will help you and others since you are what you say. God wants you to be able to find the power that is within you to succeed.

Tell God things such as "I trust you" and "I thank you." Even if you feel weak or unsuccessful, tell yourself you are strong in God. Tell yourself to be strong and to hang in there. The more you tell yourself things like this, the more you will believe them, and they will become true.

Statements like these are called affirmation statements because you are affirming yourself through words. You can post affirmation statements on your mirror in the bathroom or in an area that you will be able to see and speak them daily out loud to yourself.

Below are examples of affirmation statements:

- I am strong in the Lord.
- I am a good mother (parent).
- I am a great writer.
- I am wonderfully and fearfully made.
- I am not a quitter.
- I will become a great manager/leader.
- I will get through this challenge.

- I will accomplish my goal of becoming an entrepreneur.
- I will obtain my bachelor's degree in business.

Another important point is this: Speak and focus on what you have, not on what you don't have. While you can try to get what you don't have—and there is nothing wrong with this as it is a part of setting goals and realizing dreams—you should focus on the positive in your life and on what you do have. Instead of telling your friend, "I am so jealous that my neighbor has such an expensive car and such a big house," you could focus on the positive. Tell your friend, "I am so thankful that I am healthy, that I am able to get around well, that I have a good mind, that I have friends like you, and that I can work on fulfilling my dreams."

There is often much more that is positive in our lives than we realize. And if we focus on the positives and talk about them, we are much more likely to feel happy and fulfilled. Focusing on the negative only makes us feel worse and, as is often the case, it can drive people away from us, making them not want to be around us since all we do is complain. Our lives will be vastly improved if we realize and are thankful for what we do have.

In addition to focusing on the positives, focus also on what you are more than what you are not. In speaking about yourself with other people or to yourself, do not put yourself down. Instead, build yourself up. Focus on what is good about you as a person and who you really are. Instead of calling yourself "stupid" because you missed a turn on the highway, acknowledge your mistake but say that you are usually good about getting where you are going and that everyone makes mistakes.

While working to improve your weaknesses is a good thing, especially for someone with the mind of a champion, beating yourself up verbally is never good. If your goal is to be a painter, speak well of your abilities. If someone asks how you are at painting portraits, say that you are getting better instead of that you can't seem to get anything right when you paint a portrait. This confidence in your abilities should help you to keep improving.

Section III: Coordinate Your Mindset and Words

Earlier in *Mind of a Champion*, we discussed how important it is to keep a focused and positive mindset. We have also talked about how significant and powerful words are. Here we will examine the coordination that needs to exist between your mindset and your words if you are to have the mind of a champion.

Why does it matter if your words and your mindset are coordinated? If what you say and what you believe do not match, people may sense that you aren't genuine in one way or another. If nothing else, *you* will know that you are not being genuine in some way, and this will not help you to develop the mind of a champion and will not help you reach your goals. Alignment of words, mind, and heart strengthens your faith in accomplishing your goals.

Look at the following Scripture:

> *For as he thinketh in his heart, so is he: Eat and drink, saith he to thee; but his heart is not with thee. (Proverbs 23:7)*

As you can see here, the way you truly believe in your heart and mind is what you are. Through what you say about yourself and about your ability to accomplish something, your words reveal your mindset. You can speak something, but if your mindset and what you believe don't line up with what you say, then you are speaking in vain. There is no need to tell a loved one, for example, that you truly want to make things better in your relationship if you do not truly believe that; saying that but not feeling it is a great example of speaking in vain.

Consider this example of a man whose words and mindset do not align:

Jason has gone to an interview to be a short-order cook for a twenty-four-hour fast food restaurant. While this job is not glamourous, there is nothing wrong with it. Jason has overcome drug addictions and successfully gone through treatment. He will look for better jobs in the future, but for now this is one that he is applying for. The problem, however, is that he does not truly want this job, which is not a good thing since other jobs do not seem to be available.

When called for an interview, Jason arrived on time, was polite, and answered the questions to the best of his ability. When Jason says things like, "I really want this job," or "I will work as hard as I need to so that I can get customers' orders correct," however, because of his body language and voice tone, he gives the impression that he does not want this job and that he will not work hard to ensure that orders are correct.

The interviewer picks up on the disconnect between Jason's words and what his body language and tone of voice indicate, and decides that Jason is not a good fit for the job. If he had only conveyed genuine enthusiasm for the position and a true willingness to work hard, he would have been much more likely to get the job. In the end, while he is told that they will call him in a few days, Jason never hears back from this potential employer. (The same problem can also affect job interviews or promotions for future job opportunities and jobs requiring greater skill as well.)

On the other hand, consider this example of a person whose mindset lines up with her words:

Kim has worked at a social services agency for three years, enjoying the work that she does to help families get the resources they need. Her immediate supervisor was promoted to a higher position, so the supervisor position has opened up. Kim talked to her manager in her department and decided that she should apply for the open position. Although some people do not enjoy their job at this social services agency, Kim is not one of them. She truly enjoys working with her colleagues, supervisors, and her clients.

During Kim's interview for supervisor, the director of her department, Evelyn, is impressed by Kim's genuine responses to the questions. Evelyn can tell that when Kim says, "I really want this position so that I can help our clients get the resources they need and so that I can help our department continue to grow and improve," that she really means it. And, the truth is that Kim does feel strongly about providing excellent service to clients and about being a supervisor who can help everyone succeed. Her mindset matches up with her words. Because of her demonstrated strength as a worker and the genuine quality of her interview answers, Kim earns the promotion she sought.

Learn to speak words that will free yourself or that will help you to build yourself up, move forward, develop the mind of a champion, and reach your goals.

To give an example from Scripture of the importance of the coordination between words and mindset, consider the following verse:

> *For I know the thoughts that I think toward you, saith the LORD, thoughts of peace, and not of evil, to give you an expected end. (Jeremiah 29:11)*

God says in the Bible that the words he uses are coordinated with his mindset, which is that of thinking positive thoughts of peace toward people. If the idea of coordinating mindset and words is so important that it is how God operates, then perhaps you should realize the significance of matching up your words and thoughts as well.

Section IV: Words Are Powerful

Words are indeed powerful. You should learn to speak words that will free yourself, using them in ways that will benefit yourself and others.

There are many harmful things that words can do:
- Words can keep you trapped in your past. You can spend a great deal of time thinking about but also talking about negative

events from your past. Much time can be spent complaining about your past, talking about things you wish you had done differently, resenting people who have not been good to you, and incessantly talking about bad experiences you have had. None of this will help you to move forward; you can easily stay trapped in your past. It is certainly helpful to sometimes reflect on your past, such as dealing with past experiences and learning from your mistakes, but staying focused on it all the time will not benefit you or anyone else. And it will not help you to develop the mind of a champion.

- Words can rob you of your joy. If you maintain a negative mindset and speak in a negative manner, you can deprive yourself of joy. Instead of finding something positive to think and say about how things are going, you can always find something to complain about. Instead of being happy that you have a nice day to be outside, for instance, you could keep talking about how you wish it were ten degrees warmer or cooler. It is easy to always find something wrong, and if you do, you will deprive yourself of happiness.
- Words can steal your dreams and hopes. You might say something like, "I would love to become a professional chef, but I know I don't have the skill to do it." Right there you have given a negative dimension to your dream of becoming a chef and have all but ensured that it will never happen. The more you repeat negative statements like that, the more likely it is that the negative thing you are saying will come true. You can also

easily destroy relationships with other people by using words to hurt or insult them. Your lack of good decisions in using words can likewise destroy your professional credibility and get you fired from your job. Words are indeed powerful.

- Alternatively, there are many positive examples of the power of words.
- Words can restore your hope. If you used to say something like, "I'll never amount to anything," you can instead say, "I have many God-given talents, and I know that I can be successful." Instead of having the self-fulfilling prophecy that you will never amount to anything come, let yourself be successful by believing and proclaiming that you will be; this is a great example of the importance of the coordination between mindset and words.
- Words can revive your passion. If you want to be an artist and you used to find inspiration from looking at works of art, you might believe and say, "I no longer find art interesting. It doesn't do anything for me anymore." On the other hand, you could coordinate your mindset and words to help you feel more positive. Instead, you might first convince yourself of and then say, "I love looking at works of art. They give me motivation and inspiration as well as hope that I can progress in my career as an artist." If you mouth positive words but do not truly believe them, they will not help you. But if you work—as the prospective artist in this example—to regain your passion, your thoughts and words will definitely help you.

- Words can refuel your drive. If you want to feel motivated again, choose your words carefully to help you do so. Instead of saying and believing, "I can't do it," you could utilize self-affirmations on a daily basis and say, "I can do it!" Almost all people at some point feel their drive and motivation become lower; at these times, use words to help you rebuild your drive so that you can progress.

When using words, realize the difference between what you can change and what you cannot. Reinhold Niebuhr's Serenity Prayer is an excellent prayer to help you realize the difference:

God, grant me the serenity to accept the things I cannot change,

Courage to change the things I can,

And wisdom to know the difference.

This prayer is relevant here because while you may find yourself focusing on past negative events, for example, you should realize that doing so will not change them. You, therefore, need to be able to accept the negative things in your past and not dwell on them continually or speak of them all the time. (You may find it helpful, however, to work on your feelings about the past through therapy, for example.) It is also important that you find the courage through God to work to change the things that you can change, such as your effort toward your goals or your relationships with loved ones. Knowing the difference between these is vital to your success and contributes to whether you use thoughts and words in a positive or negative way.

In order to develop the mind of a champion, you must realize the incredible strength and power that lie behind words and then use them accordingly. As you have seen, words can truly help you to make progress toward your goals and dreams, to improve your feelings of positivity and self-worth, and to improve your relationships with family, friends, and colleagues.

In the next, and final, section of *Mind of a Champion*, let us examine the importance of speaking with faith and assurance.

Section V: Speak with Faith and Assurance

One word can lift you out of despair; thus we need to speak into our lives with faith and assurance.

Consider the following Scripture, which is a great example of the need to speak with assurance and faith:

> *And when Pharaoh drew nigh, the children of Israel lifted up their eyes, and, behold, the Egyptians marched after them; and they were sore afraid: and the children of Israel cried out unto the Lord. And they said unto Moses, Because there were no graves in Egypt, hast thou taken us away to die in the wilderness? wherefore hast thou dealt thus with us, to carry us forth out of Egypt? Is not this the word that we did tell thee in Egypt, saying, Let us alone, that we may serve the Egyptians? For it had been better for us to serve the Egyptians, than that we should die in the wilderness. (Exodus 14:10–12)*

In the Scripture above, the children of Israel spoke out of fear and a lack of faith. Instead of trusting in God, they doubted God's plan for them. We need to do the opposite, which is to speak with faith and assurance. Many people would rather die free in the wilderness trying to make it than to die in bondage.

Resist the urge to allow what you see or experience to change your thoughts into fear and doubt. Instead, keep your thoughts and your words strong and positive. Don't allow what you see to make you speak with doubt and question God. Have faith in yourself and in God and His plan for you. To remain in faith you must speak in faith, so make sure that you speak words of faith. Speak words that will lift you up.

Here are some examples of phrases that can lift you up:

- "I am better than this."
- "I would rather earn a lower salary and be able to spend quality time with my family."
- "I am extremely capable, and I can do anything that I set my mind to."

Let's look at another Scripture for an example of speaking in faith and assurance:

> *And Caleb stilled the people before Moses, and said, Let us go up at once, and possess it; for we are well able to overcome it. But the men that went up with him said, We be not able to go up against the people; for they are stronger than we. And they brought up an evil report of the land which they had searched unto the children of Israel, saying, The*

land, through which we have gone to search it, is a land that eateth up the inhabitants thereof; and all the people that we saw in it are men of a great stature. And there we saw the giants, the sons of Anak, which come of the giants: and we were in our own sight as grasshoppers, and so we were in their sight. (Numbers 13:30–33)

In the above verses, Caleb demonstrates an excellent example of speaking positively, with faith in God and assurance that things will turn out well. Caleb thought positively and then spoke honestly in that manner. The men that are with him, on the other hand, demonstrate speaking without faith and assurance. They possessed a grasshopper mindset in that they didn't have faith and assurance in God. They viewed their challenges greater than God. More importantly they viewed themselves less than. People with a grasshopper mindset see others accomplishing their dreams and goal and not themselves. I challenge you to overcome the grasshopper mindset in thinking less of yourself. So try to be like Caleb; it will get you much further.

You can't expect to be successful if you don't align your words with your desire. You can't speak doubt, negativity, and misfortunes, for those words are seeds and they will cancel out your success. A mind of a champion speaks with faith and confidence in their ability as they look to God as the source of their strength. You must eliminate self-doubting words from your vocabulary and instead use words that fuel your passion and potential.

Hopefully, through the ideas contained within this book, you have gained insight about what it takes to develop the mind of a champion. We have examined how to reframe your mind in a more positive manner, how to see past where you are now, the importance of knowing who you truly are, ways to set higher standards for yourself, how to live in a deliberate manner with determined focus, how to seize windows of opportunity effectively, and how to think and then speak in ways that free yourself.

Consider all the concepts we have discussed as a whole. If you truly grasp these concepts and utilize them in your life, you will definitely be able to develop the mind of a champion and be the best person you can be; you will see that your dreams and goals can indeed become a reality!

Author Biography

Dr. Campbell has 30 plus years of experience in Higher Education Administration

Dr. Campbell has 20 plus years of ministry experience

Dr. Campbell has 10 plus years of experience in Leadership development and consultation

Dr. Campbell is a prolific and transformative teacher and speaker

www.ingramcontent.com/pod-product-compliance
Lightning Source LLC
Chambersburg PA
CBHW071701040426
42446CB00011B/1865